FEATURES

SPRING 2025 • NUMBER 43

EDITORIAL

10

Emancipating Labour

Peter Mommsen

Why do we work? The centuries-old quest for a truly human economy.

PERSONAL HISTORY

18

Passing on the Farm

James Rebanks

A record-breaking bull showed that my daughter is ready to start taking my place.

REPORT

26

Warehouse Workers of Paris

Benoît Gautier

In de-industrialising France, a shuttle bus is workers' last link to stability.

REPORT

44

Solidarity in the Gig Economy

Ben Wray

Food-delivery workers across Europe are pushing back.

ESSAY

70

The Revival of the Cloister

Shira Telushkin

Why are so many young Catholic women becoming cloistered nuns?

ESSAY

94

Sailing with the Greeks

Adam Nicolson

At sea in a small boat, I taste Homer's kind of freedom.

INSIGHTS

ESSAY
36 The Workism Trap
No, your career is not your path to fulfilment.
Bobby Jamieson

DOERS
41 Building the Sow Shed
There's nothing quite like an ice storm to prove you've found the right work – and partner.
Brian D Miller

ESSAY
50 The Divine Rhythm of Work and Sabbath
The Bible's story of labour begins in Eden – and its ending is still to come.
Alastair Roberts

INTERVIEW
59 The Work of the Poet
Poetry makes us more fit to inhabit reality.
Christian Wiman

PHOTO ESSAY
62 The Apurímac Clinic
A truck brings medical care to remote Quechua comunities in Peru.
Maria Novella De Luca

REPORT
79 Good Cops
As my town's police chief, I want my work to focus on relationships, not statistics.
John Clair

READINGS
90 Created to Work
Dorothy L Sayers, Miroslav Volf, Leo Tolstoy, Francis of Assisi

ESSAY
104 Why I Love Metalworking
Teaching me his craft, my father showed me the value of manual work.
Norann Voll

ARTS & LETTERS

POETRY
60 The Eye
Christian Wiman

REFLECTION
68 The Solace of the Cross
Stephanie Saldaña

REVIEWS
101 What We're Reading
Boze Herrington on *Girlatee*, Alan Koppschall on *Every Valley*, and Hadden Turner on *The Apple*.

ESSAY
107 Following the Clues
Detective stories help us discover meaning in life.
Alister McGrath

BOOK EXCERPT
111 Stanley Hauerwas's Provocations
America's theologian isn't worried about the death of cultural Christianity.
Tish Harrison Warren

DEPARTMENTS

LETTERS

4 Readers Respond

FAMILY AND FRIENDS

7 America's Grow-a-Row
   Mary Grace Mangano

8 Dancing with Neighbours
   Tessa Carman

COMMUNITY SNAPSHOT

85 The Rewards of Elder Care
    At the Bruderhof, I've learned that caregiving is not a one-way street.
    Maureen Swinger

FORERUNNERS

117 Benedict of Nursia
     William P Hyland

WEB EXCLUSIVES

Read these articles at plough.com/web43.

ESSAY

Rednecks and Barbarians of France
Houria Bouteldja's latest book marks a turn from racial politics to solidarity.
Vincent Lloyd

ESSAY

Confessions of a Former Hack
A journalist finds her work at odds with her conscience.
Shelby Kearns

ESSAY

The Third Act of Work
Work was centred on the home for much of history. Now it's back.
John Fechtel

Plough
ANOTHER LIFE IS POSSIBLE

EDITOR: Peter Mommsen
SENIOR EDITORS: Shana Goodwin, Maria Hine, Maureen Swinger, Sam Hine, Susannah Black Roberts
EDITOR-AT-LARGE: Caitrin Keiper
BOOKS AND CULTURE EDITOR: Joy Marie Clarkson
POETRY EDITOR: Jane Clark Scharl
ASSOCIATE EDITORS: Alan Koppschall, Madoc Cairns
CONTRIBUTING EDITORS: Leah Libresco Sargeant, Brandon McGinley, Jake Meador, Santiago Ramos
UK EDITION: Ian Barth
GERMAN EDITION: Katharina Thonhauser
COPY EDITORS: Wilma Mommsen, Priscilla Jensen, Cameron Coombe
DESIGNERS: Rosalind Stevenson, Miriam Burleson
MARKETING DIRECTOR: Tim O'Connell
FOUNDING EDITOR: Eberhard Arnold (1883–1935)

Plough Quarterly No. 43: Why We Work
Published by Plough Publishing House, ISBN 978-1-63608-168-7
Copyright © 2025 by Plough Publishing House. All rights reserved.

EDITORIAL OFFICE
United Kingdom
Brightling Road
Robertsbridge
TN32 5DR
T: +44(0)1580.883.344

North America
151 Bowne Drive
Walden, NY 12586 USA
T: 845.572.3455
info@plough.com

SUBSCRIBER SERVICES
Unit 6, The Enterprise Centre
Kelvin Lane, Crawley RH10 9PE
T: 0800.018.0799
plough@subscriptionhelpline.co.uk

Australia
4188 Gwydir Highway
Elsmore, NSW
2360 Australia
T: +61(0)2.6723.2213

Plough Quarterly (ISSN 2372-2584) is published quarterly by Plough Publishing House, PO Box 398, Walden, NY 12586.
Individual subscription £24 / €28/ $36 per year.
Subscribers outside of the United States and Canada pay in British pounds or euros.

Front cover: Joseph Zbukvic, *Golden Harvest*, watercolour on paper, 2014. Used by permission.
Inside front cover: Diego Rivera, *The Making of a Fresco Showing the Building of a City*, mural, 1931. Photograph by Jay Galvin on Wikimedia Images (public domain).
Back cover: Joseph Zbukvic, *Master Chef*, watercolour on paper, 2022. Used by permission.

ABOUT THE COVER

Australian watercolour artist Joseph Zbukvic based this painting on a childhood memory of watching his father, uncles and grandfather working together: 'I recall the hard work and sweat it took to build these haystacks… It was a magical sight to see these men in a row swish the blades through the wet grass.'

LETTERS
READERS RESPOND

Readers respond to *Plough*'s Winter 2025 issue, *Educating Humans*. Send letters to letters@plough.com.

WOMEN'S WORK

On Alex Sosler's 'Schools for Philosopher Carpenters': I enjoyed the issue *Educating Humans*. But in the essays about and photos of schools teaching in experiential ways – head, hands, and heart – I found it often hard to determine whether girls were included equally with boys. In his conclusion, Alex Sosler, for example, says, 'The modern economy was built on the work of hands: agriculture, industry, manufacturing. We've shifted toward a head economy: accounting, management, information technology.' What is unacknowledged here is that both economies are in fact built on the largely unpaid work of women in the family and home, as well as on every aspect of paying work. One Mount Academy photo shows a young woman working in the agriculture programme, and clearly girls sing in the choir. But no curricular description includes the hands-on work where, in the adult world, women predominate: nursing, medical tech, caretaking, home maintenance, child-rearing, early childhood education, sewing or garment construction, or home nutrition.

Of course, I think girls should be included in all the curricular options that are available, but boys would also benefit as much as girls from the ones that seem not to be offered.

Priscilla B Bellairs,
Newburyport, Massachusetts, USA

SAVING LITERATURE

On Phil Christman's 'The Queen of the Sciences': As a sincere traditionalist, I agree with your stance of resistance to the false purveyors of progress and their algorithmic mining tools. But I think you fail to recognise how academe has let down the side by surrendering the language of 'the true, the beautiful, and the good.' Contemporary literary criticism mirrors the language and mindset of the nihilists mentioned in your essay – no love of literature for its own sake, just exploiting it for some dubious project of social justice in order to allege its usefulness. For this reason I admire the ending of your essay: the refusal to make a 'case for the humanities' to the nihilists. When we adopt their language and mindset, we've already lost the fight.

Raymond G Falgui,
Metro Manila, Philippines

SILVER LININGS

On Benjamin Crosby's 'Why We're Failing to Pass on Christianity': Benjamin Crosby's piece contained some excellent wisdom for (re-)Christianising those in the 21st century who think they already know what the Bible is all about. A distinct but growing category I'm starting to see in my work with Gen Z college students are those who don't know anything about Christianity (often because their parents kept them away from a faith they had stopped believing in). However, unfamiliar with the negative experiences of their parents, some of these students come to college genuinely curious to learn what the big deal is about Jesus. For them, the 'good news' isn't merely good, it's truly news they've never heard before! They tend to require more basic forms of catechism than those who grew up going to church, but they are also typically more eager to learn since it's all brand new to them. Our 'post-Christian' era certainly has its downsides, but there are some silver linings and unique opportunities as well. I'm grateful for ministers like Rev Crosby to help show us the way.

Andrew Berg, Carlisle, Pennsylvania, USA

CLASSICS AND CAR MECHANICS

On Dhananjay Jagannathan's 'Teaching the One Percent': I recently retired from a wonderful career as a pathologist. I was a biology major in undergraduate school, but was just a little shy of a minor in classics. I still read classical literature with regularity and keep a copy of Marcus Aurelius'

Meditations and a collection of Seneca's letters at my bedside. But another pillar of my education has nothing to do with a university. I worked for eight years in a car body repair shop and rustproofing business, where I rubbed shoulders with people from the inner city and Appalachia. I learned things no formal schooling can teach.

Steve Whitlatch, Cincinnati, Ohio, USA

LEARNING THROUGH PLAY

On Peter Gray's 'Let Children Play': While reading your timely and much-needed dose of humanity and common sense, I was reminded of John Dewey's *Experience and Education* and the author's focus on the unstructured nature of play, as children develop and abide by the unwritten rules of whatever game they play. Films like the *Toy Story* franchise and *Recess* speak to what many of us of a certain age knew and enjoyed: the freedom to be children interacting with other children, and what too many of today's youngsters – and their parents, for that matter – lack. May your words find lodging in the hearts of many parents and teachers.

Lloyd Conway, Lansing, Michigan, USA

On Toby Payne's 'The Green Paint Incident': Your green-hands story reminds me of my first venture with 44 nine- and ten-year-olds crowded in our very small classroom in desks that didn't accommodate creative art activities very well. Within what seemed like only a few seconds, numerous children had their own or someone else's orange paint in their hair! I believe it was my first realisation, similar to yours, that our plans aren't always their plans, but how wondrous the experience they have in spite of us. Our children need more like you.

Mary Jo Cherry, Cleveland, Ohio, USA

On 'Educating Humans': I was trained in child-centred teaching and learning through play. It was spontaneous and fun and I loved it. Then the National Curriculum for England was introduced. I accepted that perhaps there was need for more structured learning, particularly for less experienced teachers. But teaching as vocation seems to be forgotten. It has become a nine-to-four job with no thought of preparing during holidays or doing extracurricular activities. Playing in the snow at break was banned for health and safety reasons! When I left teaching, my classroom was more of a work space, with the home corner, sand and water, and craft and painting areas gone. In their place is a whiteboard linked to the computer. I remember telling one parent that what her bright little girl needed was not more English and maths but play and learning how to relate to her peers!

But I am also heartened by my neighbour's accounts of teaching in a small village school. Today I heard of two children playing for hours and sorting out their problems not by bickering but by negotiating and tossing a coin to see who would go next, without argument at the result. Perhaps change is on the way!

June Curtis, Nottingham, United Kingdom

RELIGION IN INDIA

On Jetti A Oliver's 'Religious Persecution in the World's Largest Democracy' (Plough online): As someone who has contributed poetry by invitation to *Plough* in the past, and as a practising Hindu, I was surprised to see the biased elisions and misrepresentations in this article.

Anti-conversion measures in India date back to the era in which European Christians governed it. The British Raj discouraged evangelisation after the 1857 Sepoy Rebellion in order to keep the peace. They understood that aggressive proselytisation would disrupt South Asia's delicate social weave of religious faiths. In any case, modern India's anti-conversion laws are rarely enforced. That is why some states in eastern India have been entirely Christianised; Nagaland, for example, has a higher percentage of Baptists than Mississippi.

In any case, the supposed persecution of Christians by Hindus is overstated to the point of mendacity. The Catholic Church is the second largest landholder in India, second only to the government of India itself. This is the same Catholic Church whose Portuguese adherents perpetrated the Goan Inquisition, literally torturing Hindus into conversion over the course of centuries. Dozens of shrines and temples were demolished by the Portuguese Catholics, too; the

Spring 2025

About Us

Plough is published by the Bruderhof, an international community of families and singles seeking to follow Jesus together. Members of the Bruderhof are committed to a way of radical discipleship in the spirit of the Sermon on the Mount. Inspired by the first church in Jerusalem (Acts 2 and 4), they renounce private property and share everything in common in a life of non-violence, justice, and service to neighbours near and far. There are 29 Bruderhof settlements in both rural and urban locations in the United States, England, Germany, Australia, Paraguay, South Korea, and Austria, with around 3,000 people in all. To learn more or arrange a visit, see the community's website at *bruderhof.com*.

Plough features original stories, ideas, and culture to inspire faith and action. Starting from the conviction that the teachings and example of Jesus can transform and renew our world, we aim to apply them to all aspects of life, seeking common ground with all people of goodwill regardless of creed. The goal of *Plough* is to build a living network of readers, contributors, and practitioners so that, as we read in Hebrews, we may 'spur one another on toward love and good deeds.'

Plough includes contributions that we believe are worthy of our readers' consideration, whether or not we fully agree with them. Views expressed by contributors are their own and do not necessarily reflect the editorial position of *Plough* or of the Bruderhof communities.

future Saint Xavier proudly recorded himself doing so in his letters home. In several Indian states today, Hindu temples are controlled and taxed by the government; zero Christian churches suffer such extractive exploitation and lack of autonomy.

Furthermore, many Christian-run educational institutions in India receive government funding. Some Indian states, like Mizoram, offer government scholarships exclusively to Christian students. Often government-funded Christian schools reserve seats for Christians at a far higher percentage than their share of the population – even though their funding comes from a mostly Hindu taxpayer base. Mostly Hindu tax revenue sustains the massive budget of India's Ministry of Minority Affairs (which covers all of India's non-Hindu faiths, not just Christianity). Right across secular India's borders, the Islamic Republics of Pakistan and Bangladesh have no such dedicated Ministry to protect their Hindu and Christian minorities. Regionally, there are few better places to be Christian than India – which is why India currently harbours Christian refugees from Pakistan, but Pakistan harbours no Christian refugees from India.

The largest poll ever conducted on freedom of religion in India, the Pew poll of 2021 (seven years into Narendra Modi's tenure as Prime Minister), established that 89 percent of Indian Christians feel they are 'very free to practice their religion.' For reference, a nearly identical percentage of Hindus – 91 percent – feel that way. A larger, more statistically significant difference was found when Indians were asked whether respecting all religions was 'important to being truly Indian.' 85 percent of Hindu Indians answered in the affirmative ... compared to only 78 percent of Indian Christians.

Mr. Oliver's article gives us all some insight into that gulf. Missionary propaganda has poisoned Indian Christians against a religion that has been a gracious host to Christians since late antiquity – as well as Persian Zoroastrians and Baghdadi Jews fleeing Islam. Remember that proselytisation, traditionally and to this day, does not involve simply 'selling' one's own religion through preaching and charity. It involves defaming the target religion. In India, anti-conversion laws at worst result in a fine or a few years in jail. Right across the border in Pakistan, the penalty a Christian would face for defaming Islam is death. Mr Oliver can publish his defamatory distortions while continuing to live and work, unmolested, in contemporary India; India's two neighbouring Muslim-majority countries, as any student of the region knows, are not nearly so forgiving. Until this asymmetry is noted and praised, any account of South Asia's religion and politics is incomplete.

This article's publication is particularly disheartening to witness at a time when anti-Indian and anti-Hindu sentiment is at an all-time high on social media platforms and in public policy. I believe *Plough's* nature and mission is better than this, which is why I have taken the time to write this letter. I can only hope that you share it, in its entirety, with your readers.

—*Amit Majmudar, Westerville, Ohio, USA*

FAMILY & FRIENDS
AROUND THE WORLD

Feeding Neighbours with America's Grow-a-Row

A family gardening project grows into an organisation spanning 22 states.

Mary Grace Mangano

In 2002, Chip Paillex was looking for a way to spend time with his daughter Kyra and teach her about healthy eating. The family vegetable garden they started eventually grew so much excess produce that they were giving it to family members and Chip's co-workers. When even these recipients politely explained that they couldn't take another courgette, Chip looked for other places to share his surplus. Inspired by an article in his local New Jersey paper featuring the Flemington Area Food Pantry's encouragement to farmers to 'grow a row for the hungry', Chip and Kyra donated 55 kilos of produce to the food pantry.

At the time, the pantry had mostly canned goods and boxed non-perishables. While he was delivering his produce, a woman came up to Chip and said, 'Promise me you're going to come back because this is the first time the Flemington Food Pantry has ever received fresh produce, and I need it for my health conditions. I rely on it.' Chip promised he'd be back. Several years later, in 2008, Chip incorporated America's Grow-a-Row as a non-profit organisation. It now has 30 staff members and grows 18 varieties of fruits and vegetables on 423 acres across four properties. Through farming, gleaning, and giving, the organisation (entirely privately funded) provides nutritious food and food education to those in need.

Produce is locally distributed for free at pop-up farm markets in underserved areas in Jersey City, Newark and Camden where many people don't have access to fresh produce. Chip and his staff soon realised that these communities needed not only food but education as well. Those experiencing hunger or food insecurity may not have a microwave, a full-size fridge, or more than one frying pan and a spatula. The produce itself may be unfamiliar. Culinary education, therefore, is offered for adults and youth in an on-site commercial farm-to-fork kitchen headed by the executive chef, Shauna Alvarez. In the summer, children from various cities come to the farm for a two-week programme where they learn basic culinary skills and pick food to bring home from the fields.

In addition to these local initiatives, America's Grow-a-Row widens its impact via partnerships with other regional food banks and community organisations to distribute produce throughout New Jersey, Pennsylvania, New York, Connecticut, and other areas of the Eastern Seaboard. While not a part of a food network such as Feeding America themselves, America's Grow-a-Row donates its produce to such places across 22 states.

Volunteers from local schools, churches and corporate groups are essential to this wide-ranging work. On a typical day on the farm from July through November, up to 200 people can be found harvesting the fields. During the off-season, volunteers and staff members glean additional food by driving to supermarkets and 'rescuing' food that has been deemed unfit for sale,

---

Mary Grace Mangano is a poet, writer, and professor. Her work has been published in Church Life Journal, America, Dappled Things, *and* The Windhover. *She lives in New Jersey.*

Spring 2025 7

sometimes simply because it doesn't look perfect.

America's Grow-a-Row is committed to land stewardship and sustainable agriculture, utilising no-till farming, cover crops and crop rotation to encourage growth and retain nutrients in the fields. The staff and volunteers use drip irrigation lines and integrated pest management, and they work with the local township to receive leaf mulch and other organic matter. The farm also has its own apiaries with about 2.6 million bees, whose pollination improves the apple yield.

America's Grow-a-Row began with a father and daughter's simple desire to share the (literal) fruits of their harvest. This year, the organisation is on track to donate 1.6 million kilos of farm-fresh produce, which amounts to 14.4 million servings – enough to feed a line of people that stretches 22 miles – *per day*. That's a lot of neighbours.

Dancing with Neighbours

Saying no to certain kinds of tech makes more room for living.

Tessa Carman

It started with phones. But really, it started before that. When my husband and I moved to the Washington DC area a few years ago, we were ready to do the slow work of rebuilding community ties – work we were used to as academic nomads.

Little did we know just how rich our community was about to become. Despite the twofold challenge of academic life and living in the DC area – you just start getting to know folks, it seems, and then they graduate or get a new job – we found similar-minded friends and families who also valued faith, family, books and the arts. They were eager to join us in play readings, music nights (singing folk songs from Americana to Irish), book discussions of Charlotte Mason and Ivan Illich, and read-alouds of David Jones's *Anathemata*. Some endeavours were particularly rich: one friend hosted polyphony-and-folk-music nights; a secondary school student and a college student teamed up to direct and produce an all-girl performance of *The Taming of the Shrew*, staged on a neighbourhood front porch; and a struggling Catholic parish school was revivified through a classical makeover. Other pursuits became enduring parts of community life: one family runs a small business of teaching others to grow their own victory gardens; another hosts an annual lantern walk for Saint Martin's Day; and yet another runs a non-profit home-based daycare for children with disabilities; a thriving listserv for women organises meal trains, babysitting swaps, and requests for last-minute grocery trips; and homeschool co-op moms take turns teaching nature study, watercolours, calligraphy, military history, Shakespeare and more to each other's children.

So when I opined, 'We need more neighbourly folk dancing nowadays!' I shouldn't have been surprised when one new friend

---

Tessa Carman is an essayist, poet, and teacher whose writing has appeared in The Lamp, Fare Forward, *and elsewhere. She lives in Mount Rainier, Maryland USA, with her husband and children.*

told me about the Postman Pledge crew, who were about to host their next folk dance night. Inspired by the work of Neil Postman (1931–2003), among others, the families of the Postman Pledge commit to building community bonds while also intentionally limiting their families' use of digital technology – in particular, children don't have smartphones or access to social media. And the whole family is expected to practise thoughtful limits for the sake of cultivating 'habits of presence and attention' in order to grow in the love of God and others.

This group of families began forming when children's neighbourhood friends were being given smartphones in their preteen years. Suddenly, these children were left out of the loop of their friends' communications, and some were even bullied for being phoneless.

There had to be a better way, founders Jeanne and David Schindler figured. But human beings were meant for community; they couldn't go at it alone. So the Postman Pledge group was born in 2021. The goal, says Jeanne, is 'to live as a family more naturally and celebrate all that is good and real with other families aspiring to do the same.'

Saying no to one thing means saying yes to other things. As one mum told me, while 'the group came together to reject something, namely phones for children, it is much more about being for something – a way of living out family life and friendship, seeking beauty together.' She added, 'It is incredibly encouraging to come together with other families who want to spend time making our little corner of the world more beautiful with laughter, song, dance, poetry, games and feasts.' The hope for us parents is 'to raise our children to surpass us in virtue and in any way God has gifted them.'

Last Christmas, my family carolled with the Postman Pledge families. As we went from house to house, most lights came from homemade lanterns, and some from torches. A tall student, home from college, held out his flip phone to illumine the songbook. Behind him two younger teens, one in football shorts, lustily sang 'O Come All Ye Faithful.' A younger group of boys huddled around shared sheet music. Between houses, groups of children ran down the wide streets to the next ones on the schedule. Older teenagers walked along in their own posses, singing their own carols, sometimes in harmony. Over a hundred of us were out carolling that night. At the end, we all gathered at the Schindlers' for biscuits and cider, dancing, and more carolling.

A week earlier we'd gathered for a Dickens-themed Christmas dance. Some came in costume, others simply dressed smartly. The potluck table groaned under the weight of sweet and savoury dishes (including lots of hummus). The caller wore a top hat and cravat. Three violinists played interludes during supper. On one margin of the room men congregated at the bar; on another young boys played chase. Fathers danced with daughters and mothers with sons. Some young people danced with siblings or friends, and several were teenage couples. Some girls came in Regency dresses; a mother of four glowed in a Disney-Belle-yellow dress. A few secondary school students sported black top hats. The Fezziwig chapter from *A Christmas Carol* was read between dance sets.

Dancing together is key, I think: in learning reels and quadrilles, one is also learning how to be a young lady or a young man, and how one ought to treat others with respect and grace – and with a good sense of humour. And everyone dances together (including some with toddlers in arms) in a microcosm of the Great Dance, among neighbours and among all God's creatures; between men and women, and between God and the soul.

Poet in This Issue

Born in Snyder, Texas, in 1966, Christian Wiman once described his upbringing as having been 'saturated with religion.' But after he left home his faith faded to near non-existence. He spent time teaching at several universities, and eventually became the editor of *Poetry* magazine, where he served from 2003 to 2013. A diagnosis of incurable cancer at 39 led to a renewal of faith of sorts. Wiman has authored eight books of poetry and prose, and teaches at Yale Divinity School and the Institute of Sacred Music. He lives in New Haven, Connecticut, USA with his wife and twin daughters. Read his poem 'The Eye' on page 60.

FROM THE EDITOR

PETER MOMMSEN

Emancipating Labour

Why do we work? The centuries-old quest for a truly human economy.

In the summer of 1990, after I finished year nine, my dad decided it was time I learned to work. From as young as I can remember, I'd been tagging after him in his basement printshop, and loved helping him run the offset press. But now, he said, I was ready for more. My apprentice-master would be Ullu Keiderling, a white-bearded family friend with a blue work apron, strong Teutonic accent, and keen sense of punctuality.

The 'apprenticeship' was really an informal arrangement in which I joined Ullu, a skilled craftsman, whenever I could help out on what he was doing. He showed me where he worked in the mornings: the corner of a large workshop where he built devices that aided disabled people in walking. It was an assembly job, using a standardised design and mass-produced parts, but the device was complex: bicycle wheels, casters, cotter pins, spring buttons, guide rods, and upholstered trunk and limb supports.

Several afternoons a week Ullu introduced me to his other trades. In his book bindery, he showed me how to hand-sew signatures, repair

The building of Noah's Ark, miniature from the *Bedford Book of Hours*, ca. 1423 (detail).

torn pages with Japanese tissue, and make a hardcover from scratch out of bookcloth, linen tape, hand-dipped endpapers, and hot bone glue. Or we'd go to his cobbler shop, redolent with the sharp tang of new leather. Apart from repairing shoes, we (mostly he) crafted custom-stamped belts, leather Bible covers, and his specialty invention, black cowhide braces with brass buckles that looked seriously punk.

Ullu was a patient but exacting teacher, kind if not especially talkative. (I'd later learn that some years before he'd lost two young children, and that he lived with frequent depression.) His motions as he worked were unrushed, even when jobs were piling up. He insisted on habits of returning tools to their rightful place on the board, retrieving all dropped hardware, and regularly sweeping the floor. To him, work meant honouring a discipline, not maximising efficiency.

Looking back, I can see that much of Ullu's work was repetitive, even watch-the-clock boring, as I'd learn myself several years later when I got a job in that workshop. Yet certain moments from that summer stick in my memory – moments when nothing special happened but you'd suddenly catch a thrill of fascination. You'd watch him, head bowed, intent, competent, and you'd know: here's a man who is good at his work. You'd feel a flicker of awe. This, I think, is what philosophers and theologians mean by 'the dignity of work.'

This dignity is worth keeping before our eyes in a year when, many AI researchers predict, the economic value of work will begin to decline precipitously, as machines increasingly replace humans. This, according to some forecasters, will shift even more power away from workers to the owners of capital who can buy the machines. As one recent post at the *Less Wrong* blog wonkily puts it, 'Labour-replacing AI will shift the relative importance of human vs. non-human factors of production, which reduces the incentives for society to care about humans while making existing powers more effective and entrenched.'

If this is true, much of our work may end up not being worth much.

Even so, Ullu's example suggests that there's something about work that has nothing to do with quantifiable utility. Work done well has a dignity of its own. It is a discipline that makes us more fully human.

ONE OF THE best-known celebrations of the dignity of work comes from Martin Luther King Jr's sermon 'The Three Dimensions of a Complete Life', which he preached many times in various versions and then published in his 1963 book *Strength to Love*. King argued that this dignity doesn't depend on the earnings our labour generates or the status it gains us, but rather on striving 'untiringly to achieve excellence in our lifework', even if our job is routine or menial:

> Not all men are called to specialised or professional jobs; even fewer rise to the heights of genius in the arts and sciences; many are called to be labourers in factories, fields, and streets. But no work is insignificant. All labour that uplifts humanity has dignity and importance and should be undertaken with painstaking excellence. If a man is called to be a street sweeper, he should sweep streets even as Michelangelo painted, or Beethoven composed music, or Shakespeare wrote poetry. He should sweep streets so well that all the host of heaven and earth will pause to say, 'Here lived a great street sweeper who did his job well.'

Over the decades, King's street sweeper has made countless cameos in motivational books and PowerPoints on leadership, parenting, and career advice. Just because this inspirational messaging is a cliché doesn't make it false. It finds plenty of warrant in King's sermon,

Ullu Keiderling with a grandchild in 1995.

which is filled with up-by-the-bootstraps exhortations to self-help. For example, he preaches 'self-acceptance' to his often working-class hearers, and calls on them to 'love themselves in a healthy way.' In his account, work offers a path to self-worth and fulfilment.

But here a nagging doubt arises: Is this actually what most people's jobs are like? The average worker today isn't honoured for her 'painstaking excellence', but rather is managed as a replaceable 'human resource' who depends for her livelihood on the whims of employers and market forces. King's sermon may promise sanitation workers a sense of self-worth in performing low-status labour. But that doesn't help them if they're unable to raise a family on their wages, or if their working conditions are dangerous, or if they're replaced by robots. Given that reality, his advice can sound like a counsel to accept exploitation. The dignity of work then becomes a useful tool for employers to secure tractable workers, whom it persuades to squander their most precious treasure – their 'four thousand weeks' of life, in Oliver Burkeman's phrase – to benefit the overclass.

This criticism may seem on-point for self-help in general. In King's case, however, it misses the core of his message, of which self-betterment is just one part. That's obvious to anyone with even passing familiarity with his biography as a leader in the Civil Rights Movement and Poor People's Campaign. His 'Three Dimensions' sermon lays out the vision that guided his own work.

King launches into the sermon by marshalling the Book of Revelation as a call to build a new kind of economy, one where people are not dominated by money. (His original draft of *Strength to Love* appealed for 'a deep-seated change' to 'capitalism', but his publisher, presumably nervous of provoking anti-Communist ire, cut the line.) King glories in Revelation's vision of the coming of the new Jerusalem at the end of the age, contrasting the character of this heavenly city with modern America, which lives by 'a practical materialism that is often more interested in things than values.' The new Jerusalem, he says, is a portrayal of the 'ideal humanity' towards which he urges his hearers to strive. In this city, 'the oneness of humanity and the need of an active brotherly concern for the welfare of others' will become a living reality:

> God grant that we, too, will catch the vision and move with unrelenting passion toward that city of complete life in which the length and the breadth and the height are equal [Rev. 21:39]. Only by reaching this city can we achieve our true essence. Only by attaining this completeness can we be true sons of God.

This vision of a 'complete life' goes well beyond advocating for worker-friendly policies. Though King doesn't say so explicitly, its logic would ultimately transform the fundamental relationship at the core of modern work: that between employer and employee, or (as common law bluntly terms it) between 'master' and 'servant.' The new Jerusalem of the 'ideal humanity' would seem to go beyond just striking an equitable balance between the conflicting interests of workers and bosses. Instead, in that city both parties are to become brothers and sisters, sharing not only spiritual fellowship, but practical and economic fellowship as well.

In his lifetime, King's enemies accused him of being a Marxist, a charge he was often at pains to counter, having read Marx carefully but critically as a seminary student. Communism, he wrote in *Strength to Love*, is 'cold atheism wrapped in the garments of materialism', and so 'provides no place for God or Christ.' But as it happens, King's vision of the new Jerusalem is prefigured by the young Marx of the 1840s. Then a radical in his mid-twenties, Marx had not yet fully developed the 'scientific' socialist theory now associated with his name, and still retained traces of the utopian Romanticism of his mentors. That idealistic impulse comes most clearly to the fore in his early writings on work.

Though the young Marx's thinking is too complex to trace here in any detail, it's worth highlighting certain insights on the alienation of work. Work, he writes in his *Economic and Philosophic Manuscripts*, is the 'essence of man.' In fact, work enables us to become fully human, since it is 'man's essence in the act of proving itself.' But what happens when a worker invests her 'essence' into work done for money? Her work in this case is not that of a free human being – it is not a 'free activity' – but rather is reduced to a commodity to be bought and sold on the labour market. In Marx's terms, her work is alienated.

Marx's programme, which he pursued throughout his life, was to free workers from this alienation. Despite his hostility to Christianity, this goal has theological roots, as John Hughes argues in his 2007 book *The End of Work*. After all, Marx can only condemn the alienation of 'estranged labour' in the modern world by judging it against the standard of another possible world in which work is *un*alienated. In this world, everyone would work freely, since man 'only truly produces in freedom' when 'free from physical need.' We would work not just for survival but with an excess of creativity, as an artist works, 'form[ing] things in accordance with the laws of beauty.' Work would become delight rather than drudgery.

But for Marx, this other possible world is a potential future, not anything that has ever existed in history. He is describing an age to come. Where could that idea derive from? Analysing Marx's early writings, Hughes argues that the source, mediated through other thinkers, is the Bible. It's suggestive, he notes, that the way Marx describes unalienated work is the same way Christian tradition describes God's work in creating the world.

For Marx, while the emancipation of labour was a future goal, its triumph was inevitable. The moment of liberation would arrive when capitalism collapses under its own contradictions and finally yields to communism:

> In communist society, where nobody has one exclusive sphere of activity but each can become accomplished in any branch he wishes, society regulates the general production and thus makes it possible for me to do one thing today and another tomorrow, to hunt in the morning, fish in the afternoon, rear cattle in the evening, criticise after dinner, just as I have in mind, without ever becoming hunter, fisherman, shepherd, or critic.

It's a powerfully attractive thought experiment, especially if you like hunting or fishing. And for the young Marx, the emancipation of work changes everything. It's the key to achieving a truly humane society, one in which private property, the root of 'human self-estrangement', falls away. Then, he believed, the grim Hobbesian life

The building of Noah's Ark (details).

of mutual antagonism would yield to fellowship and solidarity: '[Communism] is the genuine resolution of the conflict between man and nature and between man and man. …Communism is the riddle of history solved.' Here it's hard to miss the kinship to King's 'city of complete life' in which 'we achieve our true essence.'

But that, of course, is not the way Marxist communism played out in practice. When Bolshevik revolutionaries sought to solve the riddle of history by force, they rapidly proved what horrors result from attempts to impose the emancipation of labour at the barrel of a gun. The dream of freedom became a justification for mass murder and a dehumanising system of tyranny. The 20th century suggests that if any laws of history exist, contrary to what Marx believed, they predict not the fall of capitalism but rather the totalitarian nature of political communism.

In 1919, as news of Bolshevism's grim progress was still filtering into Germany, the founding editor of this magazine determined to build a free and co-operative life of unalienated work. Eberhard Arnold, a Berlin-based Protestant theologian and publisher, had been plunged into a crisis of conscience by the calamity of World War I, which he blamed on Christian churches' complicity in militarism and economic injustice. Joined by a broad circle of friends that included conservative politicians, military generals, evangelicals, social reformers, and anarchists, he sought answers in 'the deepest roots of Christianity.' For him, that meant rediscovering Jesus, especially his teachings in the Sermon on the Mount, which if read literally commands non-violence, love of enemies, freedom from possessions, and unlimited sharing.

Over the course of that turbulent year, as street fighting raged in trenches outside his townhouse, Arnold came to feel an intolerable tension between his desire to practice Jesus' teachings and his own life as an upper-middle-class intellectual. While remaining personally close to his establishment friends, he declared himself a pacifist and socialist, though defining those terms in a distinctively Christian way. He had studied Marxism and, through his involvement in political debates, came into contact with Communist cadres, negotiating with them to reduce their blacklist of enemies to execute if the planned revolution succeeded (it didn't). But he rejected their goals and methods, insisting that 'Christian communism' was voluntary and nonviolent: 'We do not believe in any other weapons but those of the Spirit of love which became deed in Jesus.' The new Jerusalem would be built not by coercion but rather through a spiritual revival and the organic growth of grassroots associations. Like John Ruskin and William Morris before him, Arnold imagined a network of rural co-operatives, urban settlement houses, arts and crafts guilds, social missions, and 'ancient monasteries and new Protestant orders.'

To put his new convictions into practice, in 1920 Arnold and a group of coworkers founded a small Christian community in the Hessian village of Sannerz. They planned to support themselves through farming, a children's home, and publishing. With friends, he launched a biweekly magazine dedicated to 'applications of living Christianity.' Both community and magazine bore the name *Neuwerk*: 'new work.'

The building of Noah's Ark (detail).

What was this new work? In a manifesto printed in the magazine, Arnold defined it in terms that sound almost Pentecostal:

> We have only one weapon against the depravity that exists today – the weapon of the Spirit, which is constructive work carried out in the fellowship of love. We do not acknowledge sentimental love, love without work. Nor do we acknowledge dedication to practical work if it does not daily give proof of a heart-to-heart relationship between those who work together, a relationship that comes from the Spirit. The love of work, like the work of love, is a matter of the Spirit. The love that comes from the Spirit is work.

In contrast to the young Marx, for Arnold love comes first, as the fruit of spiritual renewal. The emancipation of labour follows as a result.

Still, for both visionaries this emancipation meant removing the domination of money over human relationships through sharing all property in common. Arnold explained *Neuwerk*'s goals in a letter to supporters, pointing to the early church's practice of community of goods as described in the Book of Acts:

> For us, brotherly community of goods has become something natural, an inner matter of course. We share everything, because no other relationship is any longer possible for us. What we are concerned with is a communal economy, which is not based on any kind of mutual obligations or claims. Its basis is the free spirit of the early Christians and their common life. Not only does the land belong to all; all means of production, all materials and other goods are also common property.

In such a 'communal economy', status distinctions between different kinds of work disappear, and all work attains its fullest dignity:

> It is commonly argued that this is a utopia and that no one would do menial tasks unless compelled; but this reasoning is based on the false premise of present-day humanity in its moral decline. Nowadays most people lack the spirit of love that makes the lowliest practical job a source of joy. The difference between respectable and degrading work disappears when we nurse or care for someone we love. Love removes that difference and makes anything we do for the beloved person an honour.

As Arnold's biographer Markus Baum records, Arnold applied these words to himself. Even while running the publishing house and serving as the community's pastor, he took his turn splitting firewood and turning compost, noting the 'humanising effect' of a few hours of daily manual labour.

Over the course of the 1920s, as the Sannerz community grew to around 70 people, critics often accused it of withdrawing from society in a quest for religious purity. Arnold responded that the point was not to gather a spiritual elite. He disavowed any pretension that groups like his could fully extract themselves from the 'worldwide capitalist economy', and rejected any claim to moral heroism: 'None of us believe we are capable of creating anything better or more religious than other Christians.'

Instead, his goal was to build a practical life of Christian discipleship that was open to anyone, from homeless war veterans to single mothers to disillusioned youth. Theirs would be a small and inevitably imperfect experiment, yet still a living proof that another life is possible. 'Faith demands … that we risk and dare everything out of love in order to find new, practical ways leading to brotherliness, to a society free of discrimination, to sharing all work and goods so that personal property, and capitalism's stratification of human beings through money, are overcome.' This communal life – one in which 'work is love, and love is work' – would be a microcosm of the new Jerusalem.

Spring 2025 15

The successors to Eberhard Arnold's community and magazine still exist, having escaped National Socialist Germany in 1937 and then moved from England to South America to the United States. The magazine is the one you're holding, and the community is now known as the Bruderhof, Plough's publisher. Ullu, who still remembered Arnold from living in the German Bruderhof as a child,

According to Revelation, not just the memory of their works, but the works themselves, accompany the righteous labourers into the new Jerusalem.

had lived through much of this history by the time he taught me to bind books and make belts in year nine in a Bruderhof in upstate New York.

In retrospect, Ullu's work that summer bore an uncanny similarity to the young Marx's evocation of what unalienated labour would be like. His days alternated freely between the workshop, book binding, and shoe repair, just as Marx had fantasised about a varied schedule of hunting, fishing, and literary criticism. I realise now that this freedom resulted from the 'communal economy' that Arnold and his Sannerz friends had called into being. Ullu's work wasn't a job to him. As a Bruderhof member, he received no pay, and though he was of course accountable to the community, he had no boss. When he and his fellow old-timers were occasionally asked by visitors if they ever got a vacation, they would reply, 'Vacation from *what*?' Their work was their love, and their love was their work. 'To work is to pray', runs an old Benedictine motto – *laborare est orare* – and while that may not apply to every job, for Ullu's work it held true.

Over several weeks that June, Ullu built a circular stone wall at the entrance to the community's campus, surrounding a linden tree. It was a sweaty Hudson Valley summer, the circle was to be eight metres in diameter, and it was my job to haul the undressed stones for Ullu to fit in. When the wall was almost complete, he beckoned me over, pointing to a hidden niche he'd built into the structure. *That* was for the time capsule, he said. We collected a boxful of artifacts of that year – including, as I remember, several new Plough books – sealed them in an airtight container, and cemented it into the secret chamber for a future archaeologist, with '1920–1990' chiselled into the rock.

Ullu continued to work until a few days before he died in 2014, and his stone wall still stands, the capsule still waiting. They won't last forever, of course. Neither will the community or magazine that Arnold founded (though I hope they both still have a long run ahead of them). All human work, the 'new work' included, dies in the end, according to the Book of Ecclesiastes. 'What does man gain by all the toil at which he toils under the sun?' it asks bleakly. 'All [is] vanity and a striving after wind.'

Or is it? King's parable of the street sweeper points at another possibility. It seems that in the story the street sweeper dies. Will the hard-won dignity of his work now vanish into oblivion, as Ecclesiastes would have it? Not according to the story's ending, since his labour receives heavenly approbation: 'The host of heaven and earth will pause to say, "Here lived a great street sweeper who did his job well".' Somehow, it seems, the mark of the man's work endures.

The Book of Revelation makes the point even more plainly a few chapters before the verse King used for his sermon. In this passage, John of Patmos hears a heavenly voice instructing him, 'Write: Blessed are the dead which die in the Lord from henceforth: Yea, saith the Spirit, that they may rest from their labours; and their works

do follow them' (Rev. 14:13). According to this prophecy, not just the memory of their works, but the works themselves, accompany the righteous labourers into the new Jerusalem.

Perhaps this verse echoed in King's mind in telling his parable – from his work as a pastor, he would have known it as a staple at Christian funeral services. In any case, the biblical promise that 'their works do follow them' seems to apply to those who, like King, dare everything to build the 'city of complete life.' And for the rest of us, Revelation assures us that the same promise will apply to anyone – hunter, fisherman, critic, whatever the trade – who sets his or her hand to the new work, and performs it with painstaking excellence.

The building of Noah's Ark, miniature from the Bedford Book of Hours, ca. 1423.

Belted Galloway cattle graze on James Rebanks's farm in Cumbria, United Kingdom.

Passing on the Farm

A record-breaking bull showed that my daughter is ready to start taking my place.

JAMES REBANKS

There is an old saying in my part of the world that 'nothing much grows in the shade of a big tree.' People say it when talking about how the sons and daughters of some big-shot farmer are 'no good.' The meaning is that the father was so dominant and held on to everything for so long that the next generation didn't grow as big as it might have.

Any such comment is cruel, but that does not make it untrue.

I know a little about this saying because I grew up in the shadow of such a man, my granddad.

My granddad ruled our farm and our lives like some biblical patriarch. He was an impressive and charming character whom people liked and respected. And he was one of the most intelligent

---

James Rebanks is a sheep and cattle farmer in Matterdale, Cumbria. His first book, The Shepherd's Life, *was published in 2015. Since then, he has written several other books, most recently* The Place of Tides *(2024).*

people I've ever met. He called me his squire. He taught me how to buy and sell sheep and cattle, how to do business with other farmers, and how to manage our reputation so folk trusted and liked us, because such things matter in a small farming community. And he took me with him around the fields as the blue-eyed prince who would inherit his kingdom. I did end up farming his land and I definitely inherited some pride from him as well. His grandfather (my great-great-grandfather) had been a man who had made a lot of money and was respected locally.

I knew I wasn't the best football player at school, or even the most book smart in my class, but I could imagine being this kind of smart, field smart. So, I modelled myself on him.

A few years ago I called nearly all the shots on the farm. I was tougher, harder and more industrious than almost everyone else I knew, and I dragged my family along with me to get things done. And it worked, because being hard often does work – we got the farm, we created our flock and our herd of cattle, and I worked through the nights to write two bestselling books.

But something changed in me in the past decade: I lost interest in being that kind of patriarch. In fact, I began to actively dislike such men when I met them.

Part of this was because after my grandfather's death, 30 years ago, I had watched my father become the farmer and head of our family, and I came to admire him for becoming much more than his father had allowed him to be. Just as an oak tree crowds out its own saplings from the light, making them stunted dwarf trees, so too can humans shrink their children's spirits if they overshadow them and deny them experiences that allow them to grow.

As you get older you realise that your heroes have feet of clay. I came to see that my grandfather wasn't much of a husband, and not the best of fathers. My wife and children deserved better than that.

We have four children. They all help on the farm, but our second daughter, Bea, is the keenest young farmer at the moment. She has grown up helping me with chores on the farm, starting when she was three or four years old. She's a smart, loyal, and hard-working kid who wants to work on the farm among the cattle and sheep, and who cares about our land. I've tried to teach her everything I know. I've not met many youngsters who know so much already or are as capable. And because I've been learning a heap about soil and ecology in the past decade, she's learned a lot of that too, alongside me.

There have been two effects of this learning for me. The first is the realisation that many of the old men I looked up to didn't know a damn thing about soil health, photosynthesis, or ecology.

Farmers retiring now have spent their whole working life in the conventional farming model that emerged after World War II, a model that relied on chemicals, drugs, and mechanical solutions. We know why they did those things, and can sympathise. But many of us aren't going to do them anymore now that we know their ill effects.

Some farmers were smart enough to see the flaws in those systems, but many still hold on tight to the notion that farming intelligence ended in about 1995, and that there's nothing worth knowing after that. I have great respect for the elderly, but I've heard enough terrible arguments from old men to cure me of any illusions about all of them being wise. If anything, they are getting in the way of the youngsters on many farms, keeping them from applying new science and implementing change. The older you get the more you have invested in the status quo – your whole identity is often wrapped up in the way you farm.

A view of James Rebanks's farm with surrounding countryside.

Who's big enough to admit they were wrong their whole life?

I've had to learn a heap of painful lessons about the limits of my knowledge in the past few years and face up to how many things I was simply wrong about. I saw an old photo the other day of our farm with the sheep grazing, and it was an image of truly terrible overgrazing, every blade nibbled to the soil, unpalatable weeds breaking through everywhere, and the fields looking yellow and the sheep sick.

But there is something else. That girl of mine is going to start her farming life knowing more good stuff than I knew when I was 40 years old.

That's exciting to me. I've taken her with me to see some of the best farmers in the world. And because I happen to write books, we get a procession of smart people from around the world coming to see our farm. My kids have grown up listening to them talking about soil biology, adaptive multi-paddock grazing, and breeding strategies for functional cattle and sheep. Sometimes now I just listen as the kids swap notes with people at our kitchen table about these things. Recently Dr Allen Williams, an early pioneer of regenerative grazing, visited and the whole family got to asking him questions about grazing strategies and cell shapes and other technicalities.

Somewhere along the way I've stopped thinking this farm is about me. I've realised that's limiting and small-minded. I'm not in competition with my children for power – I want to help them get started, help them become smart learners, and let them start making the life and business decisions that you learn from, because nothing teaches you like making mistakes. We are now learning together, and it's the coolest thing I've ever experienced.

A few weeks ago, my daughter joined the payroll. Technically she is an apprentice. She has left school and goes one day a week to college to study agriculture.

On the good days we work as a team, I teach her the things I know as we work, and she soaks it up. Occasionally we fall out and have frank exchanges of views and butt heads a little. On one particularly bad day I told her she was fired, and later had to apologise for losing my temper – regular father-daughter stuff.

We spent the summer and autumn working on our first crop of bulls to sell. A few years ago, we moved into keeping a new breed, Belted Galloways. We invested in quality female genetics from some of the top herds, but it has taken a while to breed anything good enough for the society sales, not least the main sale at Castle Douglas. I'm a little lacking in cow prep skills, after years of being only a sheep man. My daughter perhaps sensed this and went last year to spend some time with Helen Ryman, a top cattlewoman with a wonderful old herd on the west coast of Scotland.

Helen was incredibly generous in taking Bea under her wing and being a mentor. Bea stayed in her home and worked with her for a week before they took cattle to the Highland Show.

Since then, Bea has taken the lead in our cattle work. Her knowledge of halter knots, combing, washing, drying and walking is better than mine, and I tend to do what she says. Several times a week we get the bulls in, tie them up, and spend time grooming and washing them, getting them to trust

The author's father with James (right) and other family members.

us so they walk quietly on their halters. We went to the Highland Show with three of our own cattle last summer and Bea learned a lot from watching the other exhibitors, many of whom also shared their knowledge. But the show ended without much success. It was a little dispiriting, despite receiving some compliments for our cattle. We learned a lot, though, about the condition needed for showing and the timing of the different stages of preparation. We told ourselves we would raise our game for the autumn bull sales.

This past October we took our first bull with some nervousness. The Highland Show had done us a favour by humbling us a little and making us work harder, so our expectations were quite modest. Once we had him tied in his pen, though, washed and blow-dried, I went for a walk down the lines to see everyone else's cattle and got a pleasant surprise. We were not only competitive, but we actually seemed to have turned him out looking like one of the better bulls in the sale. When the established breeders said we had done our job well, they clearly meant it.

The next morning was the presale show and after an hour or two of combing and making him sparkle, we took him to the showing shed. Bea led him in, a not very big 17-year-old kid gliding in with a one-tonne bull alongside her shoulder. When I got to the gate, she told me to stand back, she had it covered. The stewards closed the gate and the crowd swelled behind it. I had to stand on tiptoes to see what was happening.

Somewhere in my head I had assumed I was still needed here, at the very least to follow behind with the show stick and give the bull little prods and pats to keep him moving. But I could see Bea neither needed nor wanted any of that. For the first time since I was a child, I wasn't at the heart of the action.

Bea walked the bull like a pro, stood him when the judge wanted him in a certain place, and then

Photograph courtesy of James Rebanks.

Bea with her prize bull at the Belted Galloway Sale at Castle Douglas, October 2024.

walked him away to demonstrate his locomotion. After a minute or two the judge gestured to Bea to pull the bull into the first-place area, and then his second pick below her, and on down the line. After a minute or two of final checks, he handed Bea a first-prize rosette, and the crowd clapped. She beamed with the widest teenage smile I've ever seen. The other competitors, some of whom were also young, leaned out while holding their bulls to shake her hand. And I was leaping around behind the crowds feeling ecstatic, taking a congratulatory handshake or two from other farmers.

After the show the buyers flooded to our pen, and it felt like we had a hot piece of bovine property. Later in the day it was our turn in the auction to sell him. Bea walked him steadily around the ring and the bids kept coming. He flew to 20,000gns (£21,000), matching the breed record. Again, I was more or less a passenger, standing by the rostrum. Our wildest dreams had been exceeded, and we had laid down a marker in the breed, one we will have to live up to in the coming years.

But there was something magic about the sale beyond the high prices and the pride. Several of the leading prices were secured by family farms like ours, with teenaged or 20-something stockmen and women. There is a narrative that farmers are aging, and maybe that's what the statistics show, but it's not true in any meaningful sense. All my children are invested in the farm, and they have many friends and peers doing the same.

I no longer want to be the kind of patriarch my grandfather was. I don't need, or want, to rule my world like that. I have finally come to see such authority as limiting and more than a little selfish. It is retained only by being clutched tight and denied to others, and it makes everyone around the patriarch smaller and less fulfilled.

A little late I've learned that the wise empower those around them, giving away their knowledge and authority to make the next generation more effective.

Watching Bea lead that bull around the sale ring, I knew that something had changed. She still loves her dad, and can still learn more tricks from me, but I now know that if I were to pass away, she would be just fine, and so would my other kids. They know how to work hard, how to deal with other people, and how to advance toward goals of their choosing. They know how to be classy and kind.

I hope I live for decades more, but I already have a certain peace of mind knowing this. I imagine

my own father, dying of cancer, felt something similar when he saw that his children all had jobs, partners, and children and could navigate the world. I hope he did.

The day after the sale my daughter posted some proud pictures of the bull and its very classy handler in their moment of glory.

Who could blame her? That day was a dream for a farm kid seeking to show the world she was serious about being a farmer.

Among those social media posts was a selfie of her and me leaning over the bull, and she had written that the best thing about the day was doing it all with her best friend – and she meant me.

You can rule a family, or even a country, with fear, but to me that seems a pitiful kind of authority. When we lift up the people around us, below us, and younger than us, we build a whole that is greater than what was there previously. We are growing true wealth: happier and healthier humans and a community around us that is full of love. What other wealth is there that means anything?

James Rebanks (fourth from left), Bea Rebanks (third from right), and stockwoman Helen Ryman (far right) pose with other family members and the prize bull.

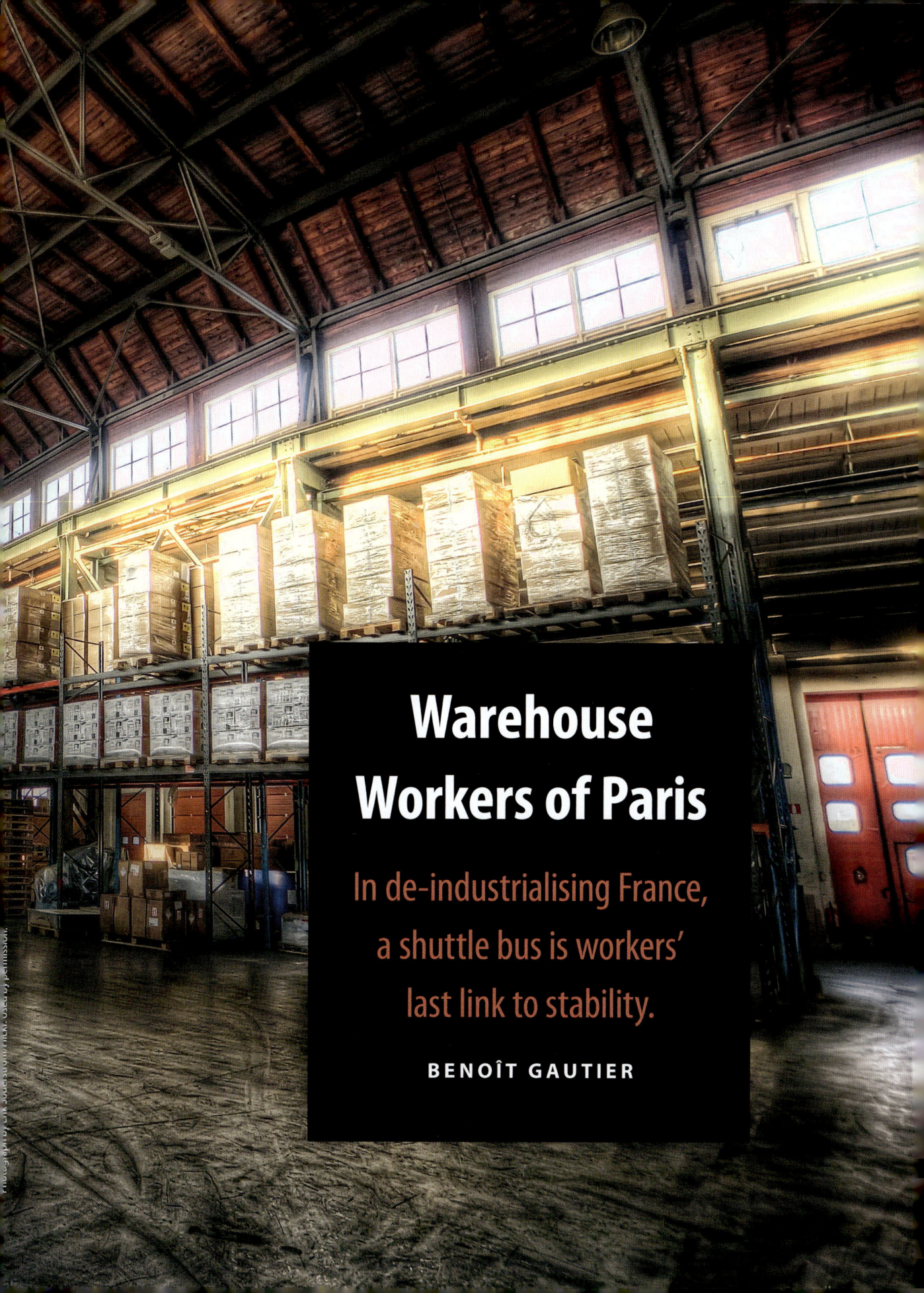

Warehouse Workers of Paris

In de-industrialising France, a shuttle bus is workers' last link to stability.

BENOÎT GAUTIER

The Batignolles, in the 17th arrondissement of Paris, used to be an industrial neighbourhood. Walk there now and you'll see a mix of chic, quirky boutiques and new social housing. A century and a half ago, in the romantic little park you'll spot lying behind the Sainte Marie des Batignolles church, prisoners taken from the fallen barricades of the Paris Commune in the area were gathered, shot, and thrown into a mass grave. It is said they still lie there, in that romantic little park, somewhere under the music pavilion. Go down from the church, cross through the park, and you'll find a small train station. Standing there, a century ago, you would see mile after mile of warehouses. Then, the railways connected Paris with France's industrial northwest, and beyond that the factories of Great Britain.

Today, like much of French industry, the warehouses of the Batignolles have nearly all moved away. Twenty years ago, in the early 2000s, one warehouse – owned by a menswear company – was still clinging on, a link in the logistical chain carrying stock to retail stores all over the country. When I first met the man I'll call Kwasi through my work for his trade union, he told me how he started working for the company back then, moving to a flat in the Batignolles' social housing blocks not far from the warehouse. Right at the limits of the city but still just inside the walls of Paris, his flat was even then a rare luxury for any low-wage industrial worker. Almost two decades later, he is still living in the Batignolles, along with a dozen other warehouse workers. The warehouse itself is gone.

A few years after Kwasi was hired, management said it couldn't afford Parisian rents, so it moved the warehouse a few miles out of town, to a densely populated working-class area in the city of Épinay-sur-Seine. I hop in Kwasi's car for the ride; half an hour later, we get out where the warehouse was moved, next to a cemetery in Épinay. At the time of the move, workers living in the Batignolles had to take the train to work at the new location, while others were hired from those living nearby. The workforce began to look more like the population of Épinay: black and brown people whose families came from Africa, the Caribbean, or the Indian subcontinent.

But operations had to expand, costs had to shrink, and – although Épinay wasn't exactly a high-end real estate area – everything had to move again, even further away from Paris. Now the warehouse is several hours' drive to the north, in the Picardy region: a flat land of crops, thinly populated by working-class whites. And again, management hired new workers from among people living nearby. The warehouse's walls came to contain three very different types of workers. There was a scattering of the final generation of industrial working-class Parisians, the childless heirs of the communards buried in the romantic little park. The workers from Épinay, sometimes called *banlieusards*, are often recent immigrants, taking their nickname from densely populated projects on the outskirts of Paris, the *banlieues* – known for episodic rioting, often triggered by police violence. And lastly, the working-class whites of Picardy, who lived in semi-rural communities spread out on the plains, far away from the cultural centres: their employment was dependent on car ownership and their economic equilibrium hinged on the price of gas. These are the people who protested in the streets in 2018 and 2019, during the 'yellow vests' revolts.

The *banlieusards* never joined the yellow vests in great numbers, and the working-class whites never showed any significant support for the struggles against police brutality in the banlieues. The two groups are so different – in their culture, interests, and day-to-day lives – that the left-wing political

---

Benoît Gautier is a writer and translator living in Paris, France. He contributes regularly to Études *magazine, and compiled and translated the first anthology of Herbert McCabe's work in French.*

parties have trouble building a coalition with which both strands of workers could identify. To some on the left, uniting 'those of the towers and those of the towns' is the ultimate political goal. Others think these aspirations are just a fantasy. Even when the two groups are doing the same work, as in the warehouse, their demands on management often diverge: where banlieusards would like help with childcare or public transport costs, their white co-workers prefer higher wages to spend on gas. It would be very easy to assume that these people do not belong to the same working class.

When they heard about the warehouse moving again, some of the workers living in Batignolles and Épinay simply left for another job. Many who remained stayed because they had no other choice: they were too old to reenter the job market, or their bodies had been beaten down by the work, or they were single women with children to feed at home. The workers from Batignolles and Épinay bargained with the company for a free shuttle leaving from the warehouse's old site in Épinay to their new workplace out in the fields of Picardy.

When I get on the shuttle, Kwasi introduces me to the passengers. My line of work – union-appointed expert in health, safety and working conditions – only exists because of a few paragraphs in the *Code du Travail*, the thick compendium of French labour laws. They were inserted in the code by a socialist government in the early 1980s. It was the culmination of a movement as old as industrial capitalism, advanced over decades by a coalition of left-wing politicians, Catholic social activists, labour sociologists, and progressive managers. These people believed that working life had to become more democratic, that

bosses and workers had to enter into dialogue about how to regulate the workplace, and that, if this could be enforced, a new type of society would emerge. Some envisioned a stabilised, ethical capitalism; others, a socialism defined by workers' self-management from below.

One of the requirements in the *Code du Travail* is that workers' representatives should be able to call for the help of experts, so they could debate with the bosses – and their armies of hired consultants – on a slightly more equal footing. In 1981, some commentators warned voters that Russian tanks would parade down the Champs-Élysées the day after the election of a socialist president. The tanks never showed up. People like me did instead: inviting themselves into factories, opening the workshop doors, encouraging usually silent workers to talk about their experiences, demanding managers answer questions that made them angry and uneasy.

The people I meet in the warehouse shuttle are mainly black and brown women. They have no cars: most have already ridden public transportation for an hour or more just to reach the shuttle. From Épinay, it takes more than another hour to get to the warehouse. On the shuttle, the women – and a few men – tell me how the commute eats up almost all their free time, making it difficult for them to care for their children, who seem to be the main motivation to continue working a gruelling, dangerous job.

Rolling up their sleeves, a few of them show me scars running from their wrists to their elbows. The quick, repetitive movements of their work at the warehouse wear out their nervous systems and over time, cause partial paralysis of their hands. Some of them have had the same injuries three or four times, multiplying the scars. The medical procedures to patch up arms and hands are too slow to heal to match the rhythm of the machines they work alongside. Laughing, these women tell me about the time one colleague had a finger cut off by one of the warehouse's machines: 'We never found it, it must be in a box somewhere in a store.' They point me to a man sitting in the back of the bus, who obliges us with a wave of his four-fingered hand. He does not laugh about it like his workmates do. I think about this guy's mummified finger, perhaps sitting in a box of low-rise jeans, somewhere in logistics purgatory, still waiting to be found.

Kwasi wanted me to ride with his colleagues, to hear directly from them: to see their faces, their arms and hands. I am here because the company claims it can't afford the shuttle anymore. Kwasi hired me and a colleague to show the consequences this choice would have on the workers, and hopefully, to convince the company to abandon its plan.

One of the guys here, an older man with a thick Greek accent, takes my phone number. He tells me he wants to meet in person. He says he has documents that prove the company is not acting in good faith. We meet in one of the last working-class bars in the Batignolles area, near where he lives, just in front of the train station. Over his shoulder, I can see the music pavilion of the romantic park. He shows me the documents. Maybe he guesses from the look on my face that what he has given me is not nearly enough to change the company's decision, because his hands grab my arms, pleading, with visible anguish, for me to 'save the shuttle', as if this little bus is the last thing holding his professional life, and maybe his life in general, together. On his face I see the vulnerability of these workers to decisions about their lives, made without them, over which they have no control.

As an expert on worker safety, I was appointed by the unions to go talk to workers on the shop floor, ask them about their troubles, and look at the conditions they were working in. Most of the time, the workers didn't have a problem with our presence there, or our questions. Managers did. They found our inquiry intolerable; all the more so because, by law, the company had to pay for it. They wanted to know, and even have a say in, who we met, what questions we asked, where we went, and what we saw. They agreed that workers' safety and well-being were important topics, that they were happy to hire experts to help them understand problems and reduce risks. They weren't happy that the experts they got were us. Seeing how nervous we made managers told me my presence was more

---

Entering the warehouse, I see the rapid movements of the conveyor belt workers who fill the packages, watching them silently wearing out their nervous systems. I feel the unbearable temperatures in the lorries where young guys pile heavy packages.

---

than a piece of bureaucratic red tape. Unusually for them, there were decisions being made in their workplaces which weren't on their terms. It was Kwasi who decided that the choice to scrap the shuttle had to be investigated, that my colleague and I would be the experts to investigate it, and that we started our inquiry by talking not to the company but to the workers themselves.

Spring 2025

Entering the warehouse, I see the rapid movements of the conveyor-belt workers who fill the packages, watching them silently wearing out their nervous systems. I feel the unbearable temperatures in the lorries where young guys pile heavy packages. Management has told us not to worry about them: all packages are weighted, the weight carefully managed, to ensure the work never meets the legal standard of 'hard working conditions' (which would oblige the employer to offer early retirement). One of the workers shows us how the scale weighing their packages has been tampered with, containers always measuring as lighter than they really are. On paper, and in company policies, French labour law makes workers here better protected than anywhere else in Europe. On the other hand, France is one of the most dangerous countries for workers in the European Union: it's the fourth deadliest and the most accident-inducing. In my visits to shop floors, warehouses, and many other workplaces, it is clear why: the laws and regulations are rarely applied in full, controls are rare, and when employers are caught red-handed, the fines are modest and their amount is capped by law.

We talk to forklift operators whose spines are deformed from years of constantly looking upward to the giant shelves where the product is stored. One of them, hired three or four years ago in one of the rural white communities local to the last stop in the warehouse's travels, tells me she's had two spine operations because of work-related injuries. Sports were an important part of her life when she first took the job, but she has had to leave all that behind. However, she is grateful that the managers didn't throw her out after they ruined her back – and she has no sympathy for the shuttle people, or any attempt by the union to defend those (to her mind) vindictive *banlieusards*.

After a month of investigation, and some 40 interviews with workers, another union-appointed expert and I go from the lorries and conveyor belts of the warehouse to a windowless room in the menswear company's headquarters. Facing us are the workers' representatives and the company management, headed by a human resources manager who specialises in labour relations. We are there to

---

It's a simple story: work moves with capital. If that's the way things must go in the end, why couldn't we go along to get along and spare ourselves the drama, the anger, and the screams?

---

present the results of our study about the shuttle and the working conditions of those who use it. As the PowerPoint slides light up behind us, we talk about the twisted spines and the rigged scales, the high temperatures and the eroded nerve endings. We try to show how the shuttle is a central piece in a fragile equilibrium keeping the lives of its users together. We provide evidence, pictures, statistics and verbatim quotes.

In our report, we set down on paper words from the workers that higher-ups in the company would never otherwise have to consider or even see. A lofty conference room where board members usually meet to talk about work in abstract, esoteric language – costs, growth, market shares, return on investment – hosts a presentation filled with facts and figures that speak of an inconvenient reality. The company can still shut the shuttle down after we've finished our work. But it can no longer claim

to have no idea about the consequences. And if, one day, the untenable pressure their decision has placed on their workers' lives results in someone's injury or death, our report could become a decisive piece of evidence in a criminal court.

We stay six hours in that room. Much of this time is spent shouting. One of the executives doing most of the shouting – shouting till he is red in the face, till he has literal foam at the mouth – is the head of HR. The others take it in turns, interrupting our responses, disparaging our research, telling us that none of what we are telling them is true. While the lead of the management team, the specialist in labour relations, isn't competing in the shouting match, he is playing with a sheet of paper, smiling. He holds it so we can read the contents during our presentation. It is a letter informing us that we are being sued for excessive use of our licence to investigate working conditions. The letter will never be sent. It is just a way to mess with us during our presentation while telling us to play nice.

We have to maintain a face of neutral expertise over these hours of intense and chaotic exchange. Our report relies on the assumptions written into the *Code du Travail* all those decades ago: that presenting convincing evidence to reasonable people will lead to progress on goals they profess to hold in common, like protecting the health of workers.

What makes these six hours of shouting even more of an ordeal is that everyone in the room recognises that nothing my colleague and I say or do can ultimately stop the company from scrapping the shuttle. We can point out how detrimental that and other decisions would be to

Spring 2025 33

the workers' health and wellbeing, but we can't give those workers – the older man in the bar, the women from the banlieues with children to feed, the people in the warehouse with broken spines and faulty scales – the power over their own lives that these decisions represent.

From the company's point of view, it must all seem like a terrible waste of time and energy. Why should anyone toil to ask questions with no real chance of receiving a positive answer? What's the use of giving voices to those workers who are already on the way out? Even some of the workers from the new location see the shuttle crowd as unreliable and not productive enough.

Shutting down the shuttle is not only a way to save a modest amount of money, but also an easy way to detach from workers who are increasingly tired, old, wounded and socially disconnected from the rest of the workforce. Getting rid of the annoying old faces could even be a way to tighten the solidarity between the more recently employed and their employer. The old employees are a visible reminder that the commitment an employer promises to a community only goes so far. It is in the interest of the company for workers to imagine their contracts could last forever, since people invest themselves in their jobs when they feel they are in a long-term relationship with the company that hired them. That belief is useful until the last minute before the company moves on. It's a simple story: work moves with capital. If that's the way things must go in the end, why couldn't we go along to get along and spare ourselves the drama, the anger, and the screams?

As personally gruelling as it is to endure hours of shouting, three things sustain me: the support of my colleague, the seriousness of the work we produced together, and most importantly, the fighting spirit of the workers' representatives, who do not hesitate to stand up to management, when our official neutrality forbids us to do so. They are used to standing up for each other, in boardrooms in the angry HR manager's living room than in the shuttle among workers showing me their scars. But after I leave the windowless room, the thought of spending time with a person like him seems obscene. Solidarity is not about kin, tribes, or shared culture. It's about who you choose to serve, who you stand with, who you're willing to stand up to. Capital wants to move smoothly and

---

Solidarity is the only force that can hope to push back against power and money. It is not about kin, tribes or shared culture. It's about who you choose to serve, who you stand with, who you're willing to stand up to.

---

but more often on the factory floor. To some, they are likely annoying old faces, people who never cared too much about being liked, who don't let gratitude for good treatment give a pass to bad.

This kind of solidarity is the only force that can hope to push back against power and money, even if, nine times out of ten, the effort fails.

Those few lines in the *Code du Travail* might not have created the society their framers dreamed of, but they succeeded in a way they hadn't foreseen. The law forces management to consider the consequences of its decisions on workers' lives – to consider the voices of workers themselves. Through the work of legislators and social scientists, stories that would have remained rumours or opinions shared by a handful during coffee breaks are recorded in black and white, heard in conference halls and boardrooms. In the words and statistics of reports, workers who otherwise would be long gone and forgotten hang around, creating an unusual kind of solidarity.

For our part, socially speaking, skilled knowledge workers like my colleague and me have far more in common with these managers than the workers we have come to speak for. Before all this, I would have felt far more at home

silently, muffling the cries of the workers it uses and throws out. A façade of empathy makes the process more efficient, but the smiles quickly fade when you cross an invisible line.

This is what solidarity feels like to me: not warmth and close companionship but naked vulnerability and cold fear. Breaking through the wall of bland PR language corporations use in self-description felt like waking up into a recurring nightmare of mine: I'm strapped into my seat in a shuttle bus, empty but for me and a driver whose face I can't see. I can feel him start the engine, but I don't know the direction or the destination he has in mind. As he picks up speed, I watch helplessly as the landscape around us begins to change into something horrifying. My instinct is to try to force open a door and jump out unnoticed. From the dangerous realities of work that shuttle might be driving to, there's no such escape. But even when it feels like it, we're not alone. Look around, and the shuttle is full of passengers just like you and me. Enough to force the driver to reveal his face. Enough, maybe, to break his rules, to take the wheel and pull the emergency brake.

BOBBY JAMIESON

The Workism Trap

No, your career is not your path to fulfilment.

No matter how much you love your job, it doesn't love you back.

Schools and TV shows, mentors and bus stop ads, politicians and celebrities all proclaim that we should do the work we love and love the work we do. And we don't just love our work: we devote ourselves to it, build our lives around it, give up more and more for it. As Derek Thompson of the *Atlantic* puts it:

> The economists of the early 20th century did not foresee that work might evolve from a means of material production to a means of identity production. They failed to anticipate that, for the poor and middle class, work would remain a necessity; but for the college-educated elite, it would morph into a kind of religion, promising identity, transcendence, and community. Call it workism.

Thompson defines workism as 'the belief that work is not only necessary to economic production, but also the centrepiece of one's identity and life's purpose.' A member of my church recently said to me, 'At the consulting firm where I work, there's a sense of, what else are you going to give your life to?'

As it has been for so many religious movements, America is the hotbed of workism. Among large nations with comparable levels of productivity, none averages as many hours of work per year as America, and the gap is growing. Samuel P Huntington summarises: Americans 'work longer hours, have shorter vacations, get less in unemployment … and retire later than people in comparably rich societies.' By 2005, the wealthiest 10 percent of married men in America worked the longest average working week. And a 2018 research article found that, compared to women who graduated from lower-ranked schools, women who attended elite, selective universities do not, on average, earn more per hour, but they do work more. For women, it seems, the benefits of an elite diploma are more time at work and lower chances of marrying and having children.

Derek Thompson again: 'In the past century, the American conception of work has shifted from *jobs* to *careers* to *callings* – from necessity to status to meaning.' Drawing a longer arc, the historian Mary S Hartman has observed that in the modern era, work has become 'the chief repository of male identity.' And not just male. Camille Paglia pronounces a dire verdict on a substantial swath of contemporary feminism:

> In my opinion, second-wave feminism, for all its professed concern for mainstream, working-class, or disenfranchised women, has drifted toward privileging the concerns and complaints of upper-middle-class career women, who seek the lofty status and material rewards of an economic system built by and for men.

In America today, men and women alike adhere with growing devotion to what Scott Yenor calls 'the career mystique – a set of ideas that tries to convince men and women that changing the world through their careers is the paramount path to fulfilment, growth, and happiness.' What happens when work becomes the chief repository

What happens when work becomes the chief repository of identity, the prime source of status and reward, the paramount path to fulfilment?

of identity, the prime source of status and reward, the paramount path to fulfilment? What happens is failure that we are poorly equipped to acknowledge, much less respond to fruitfully. What happens is 'collective anxiety, mass disappointment, and inevitable burnout.' What happens is that our worship of work is shown and seen to be what the author of Ecclesiastes calls *hevel*, absurd.

'WHAT DOES MAN GAIN by all the toil at which he toils under the sun?' (Eccles. 1:3). The question opens Ecclesiastes' investigation into all of life. Toil is the engine of expected gain. And the negative answer that the protagonist, Qohelet, returns – 'no gain' – proves that, since toil is *hevel*, all is *hevel*.

By 'toil' (Hebrew *'amal*), Qohelet means roughly what we mean by 'work', typically with a negative tint. Elsewhere in the Old Testament the word can mean 'distress' or 'anguish', even 'misfortune' or 'disaster.' In Ecclesiastes, *'amal* typically means 'labour' tainted by frustration or futility. But it also names the fruits of labour: not just the money made from selling milk but the whole thriving farm that has taken

---

Bobby Jamieson is a pastor, scholar and the author of Everything Is Never Enough: Ecclesiastes' Surprising Path to Resilient Happiness *(WaterBrook, 2025), from which this essay is adapted. He lives in Chapel Hill, North Carolina, USA with his wife and four children.*

decades of sleep-stealing work to cultivate.

What does a person gain from all this work, and even from its fruits and profits?

Ecclesiastes is the record of Qohelet's systematic exploration of potential sources of pleasure and profit. In his experiment embracing all of life, work features prominently.

> I made great works. I built houses and planted vineyards for myself. I made myself gardens and parks, and planted in them all kinds of fruit trees. I made myself pools from which to water the forest of growing trees … I had also great possessions of herds and flocks, more than any who had been before me in Jerusalem. (Eccles. 2:4–7)

Here Qohelet reproduces his résumé. He describes the work of establishing a business and a household, from which and in which he could live in luxury. We should picture an ample, carefully conceived, skillfully developed estate. Qohelet's accomplishments were built to last. As Old Testament scholar Stuart Weeks comments, 'Qohelet's business is not ephemeral, and he makes his wealth not from, say, buying low and selling high or from providing services, but from vineyards, orchards, timber and livestock.' In fact, his operation is in some measure self-sustaining: pools, water, orchards, and timber groves; timber furnishes building material. Neither the orchards and irrigation, nor flocks and herds nourished by them, nor grand dwelling at the centre were apt suddenly to vanish. All will likely outlast him.

So far, so exceptionally successful. But, after cataloguing his enjoyment of other pleasures his wealth could purchase and his leisure permit, Qohelet declares, 'Then I considered all that my hands had done and the toil I had expended in doing it, and behold, all was absurd and a striving after wind, and there was nothing to be gained under the sun' (Eccles. 2:11). Qohelet here appraises not just his labour but its outcomes, and not just his wealth but the infrastructure of his fortune, which will generate more fortune. What did his work and his work's outputs do to deserve this derogatory label of 'absurd'? At the very least, their problem is not so much them as him, not that they will disappear but that he will. They'll last a while yet; he won't, much longer. The

'Better is a handful of quietness than two hands full of toil and a striving after wind.' —Ecclesiastes 4:6

problem with even lasting success is that it can't last long because its agent and beneficiary won't. Yet, as far as we can discern, Qohelet denounces his work's harvest with plenty of breath left in him. This seems to suggest a deeper contradiction.

By calling his life's work *hevel*, Qohelet asserts a standing rupture in the chain that joins desire, effort and outcome. He calls work 'absurd' because of the disparity he discerns between what he put in and what he got out. But surely his work had gone as well as he could reasonably have hoped. Whence then the divorce between what he wanted and what he got? Somehow even striking success left him wanting something more.

Shortly after this judgement, Qohelet gives two more reasons why work is absurd:

> I hated all my toil in which I toil under the sun, seeing that I must leave it to the man who will come after me, and who knows whether he will be wise or a fool? Yet he will be master of all for which I toiled and used my wisdom under the sun. This also is absurd. So I turned about and gave my heart up to despair over all the toil of my labours under the sun, because sometimes a person who has toiled with wisdom and knowledge and skill must leave everything to be enjoyed by someone who did not toil for it. This also is absurd and a great evil. What has a man from all the toil and striving of heart with which he toils beneath the

sun? For all his days are full of sorrow, and his work is a vexation. Even in the night his heart does not rest. This also is absurd. (Eccles. 2:18–23)

By definition, the person to whom Qohelet will leave the legacy of his labour did not work for it. Worse, Qohelet can't guarantee a fitting successor. The more successful you are, the more you will leave in the hands of a successor of uncertain character and competence. Both toil and wisdom are irrelevant to inheritance. Even if you're an executive who can select your own replacement, you can't control what's done with your enterprise when you're gone. Time alone will tell you whether you chose wisely – only you won't be around to hear. Death stops ambition short. What's beyond your time is beyond your control.

Qohelet's second reason is that work is full of pains. He piles up those pains like stacks of unread emails and unanswered voice messages: toil, yearning, sadness, anxiety, sleepless nights. He bemoans hardships that are not physical but psychological. Nothing human was foreign to him; long before our age of anxiety, he knew and named the malady.

In another passage on work, Qohelet stirs some proverbial wisdom into his empirical observations.

Then I saw that all toil and all skill in work come from a man's envy of his neighbour. This also is absurd and a striving after wind. The fool folds his hands and eats his own flesh. Better is a handful of quietness than two hands full of toil and a striving after wind. Again, I saw an absurdity under the sun: one person who has no other, either son or brother, yet there is no end to all his toil, and his eyes are never satisfied with riches, so that he never asks, 'For whom am I toiling and depriving myself of pleasure?' This also is absurd and an unhappy business. (Eccles. 4:4–8)

The Hebrew at the start of this passage is difficult. Most translations and commentators take it to say that all effort and achievement arise from

Spring 2025 39

envy, but a good case can be made that the verse instead ascribes ambitious work to a passion that draws one person away from another. If you stumble at the 'all', remember that it's hyperbole. Like a stand-up comic, Qohelet knowingly keeps qualifications and counterarguments out of the frame, and then squints at the resulting picture to bring one aspect into sharp focus. Whichever translation we opt for, Qohelet's point is that work is a fertile field for self-destructive desires to take root, go to ground and spread wide.

Whether fuelled by envy or self-isolating obsession, if work is the consuming passion in your life, what could it consume? What will be left after the fire cools?

When Qohelet commends a little quietness over a lot of striving, he is saying that there are limits to what work will give you, so there should be limits to what you give work. If you try to grasp gain with two hands, both will come up empty. There is no contentment without knowing and submitting to limits.

Speaking of limits, the last part of the passage profiles someone who doesn't have any, as many modern workers boast. He has no one else to work for – no partner, no heir – yet he never stops working. Sounds like so many single city-dwellers for whom work is life and life is work. Not only does he never stop working but he never asks, who for? He never asks who gains from his giving up everything in order to give it all to his work.

Who does the religion of workism benefit? If you have no dependants or heirs, then, by definition, not them. Your workism may benefit your boss. It might especially benefit your boss's boss's boss and the shareholders. But does it benefit your neighbour? Does it benefit you?

M**y wife, Kristin,** is both a foodie and a homebody. She enjoys good food and is happy to cook it, but she doesn't much like going out for dinner. So in the past few years we've settled into a relaxing, rewarding Friday night ritual. We get the children fed and in bed (or at least in their rooms) early, then cook together. Dinner, dessert, decaf espresso, conversation throughout – Friday night helps us stitch back together what the week has tugged apart.

I'm a pastor, and some of my hardest and happiest work is preaching. I spend 15 to 20 hours preparing every new sermon. In weeks when I'm preaching, I do all I can to have my sermon manuscript written, practised, and revised by Friday at 5:30pm. The deadline motivates and liberates. I don't want to mess up date night or mangle the weekend. All week, the weight of the sermon sits on me as I prepare it amid counselling appointments and phone calls and other teaching and last-minute needs and neglecting my inbox.

Once the sermon is ready late on Friday, my shoulders rise in response to the lifted-off load. I feel like I just woke up from a full night's sleep. I'm suddenly more talkative than I've been all week. And Kristin gets to enjoy (what I hope is) the benefit of (what should be) my undistracted attention.

On Sunday I have serious work to do. But from Friday at 5:30pm through Saturday night, I do my best to rest with my family. That rest can involve a daunting amount of chores and cleaning and laundry, but it also makes room for hikes and playground time and leisurely library visits.

If you want to keep work from ruling your life, set limits to its domain. Confining work keeps it from strangling and devouring everything else that gives life meaning. Commenting on the Jewish practice of Sabbath, Abraham Joshua Heschel reflects, 'There is a realm of time where the goal is not to have but to be, not to own but to give, not to control but to share, not to subdue but to be in accord.' Happiness comes not from working yourself raw, but from knowing when and how to rest.

Excerpted from *Everything Is Never Enough* by Bobby Jamieson. Copyright 2025 by Bobby Jamieson. Published by WaterBrook, an imprint of Penguin Random House, LLC. Used by permission.

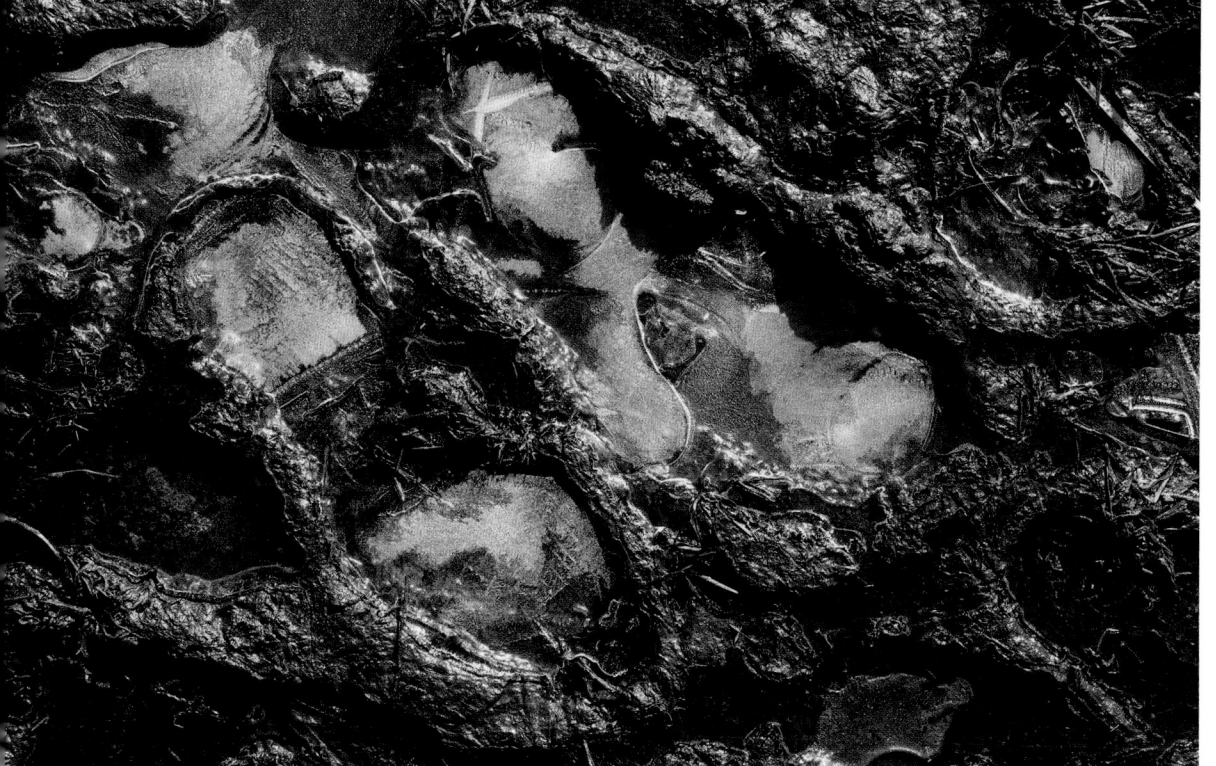

Building the Sow Shed

There's nothing quite like an ice storm to prove you've found the right work – and the right partner.

BRIAN D MILLER

Forget taking the magazine quiz 'Are you and your mate a good match?' I suggest instead that you and your beloved go outside and build a sow shed together in the freezing rain, as it coats the tools, the wood, the metal roofing, and both of you in a thin layer of ice. That should determine pretty quickly your compatibility and the mettle of your relationship. Trust me, I know.

A blowing, biting, freezing rain is what we're working in on this particular day. A real Alberta Clipper, the system arrived with full force right off the northern plains into our small East Tennessee valley. It's mid-morning, two hours since we headed outside to work, and the mercury has not budged from the -2º Celsius of sunrise. Squalls of horizontal icy rain alternate with spitting snow, ripping across the pastures and our faces at stinging speeds. The sun makes a brief appearance before wisely ducking for cover.

My beloved suggests we do the same, so we break for the house and a cup of hot tea. We are under a tight deadline, hustling to finish building a three-sided shelter before a new, very pregnant sow

---

Brian D Miller has farmed in East Tennessee USA since 1999. He and his partner, Cindy, raise sheep and hogs. He is the author of Kayaking with Lambs, *and writes at his Substack:* Notes from an East Tennessee Farmer.

Spring 2025 41

is delivered tomorrow. Much as we might prefer it, this is one project that cannot be put off for a sunny day.

When we moved to our 50-acre farm a quarter of a century ago, I set for myself a personal work goal: *Find joy in doing the everyday.* I jotted the goal down on a scrap of paper and taped it above my desk. It is a written injunction whose achievement at times has felt idealistic – especially on mornings like this, as we find ourselves together at the top of a wind-pummelled hill pasture, trying desperately to keep our fingers and toes and faces from freezing in our scramble to erect the farrowing hut before the sow decides to give birth.

When you take up farming, the work has a way of seeping into every aspect of the idyllic rural life you might have imagined yourself leading.

The tea break has come at a good time. The mood out in the field had been quickly deteriorating into one of sullen irritation. (This can happen, of course, even in the strongest of relationships.) Truth be told, though we both love being outdoors and working hard, even in inclement weather, this morning's ice and wind have been particularly wearing on the spirit. Break over, we leave the comfort of our home and return once more to the pasture, where it is now, thankfully, snowing ... for a moment anyway, before the freezing rain starts again. At this point we begin to laugh, giddy almost, at the work still to be completed amid these uncooperative elements.

When you take up farming, the work – both the doing and the thinking about it – has a way of seeping into every aspect of the idyllic rural life you might have imagined yourself leading. It occupies most waking moments, every day, week, month, and year. Sitting in your easy chair dreaming about the 'simple life', warm and comfortable with a book and a glass of whiskey is one thing. It is altogether something else to be coated in ice, getting on with the job at hand because you have no other choice.

To be clear, all of us nestled in the bosom of 21st century modernity do have some choice in how our years get spent, and my beloved and I wholeheartedly chose this work, this farming life. To the man with the 'finding joy' reminder scribbled above his desk, that means that if one day he finds himself with an ice-coated hammer in one hand and a clutch of 10d nails in the other while his partner waits with the next rough-cut oak board to be nailed and another angry squall rains frozen misery down on their heads, he should try, as hard as it may seem in the moment, to factor a little enjoyment and satisfaction into the work. He has been able to do so on most days, and today will be no different.

We continue working throughout the day on the solid eight-by-ten-foot structure, breaking only for lunch (a quick bowl of tomato soup and a grilled cheese sandwich) and the occasional dash to the barn. Though the wind is still coming hard from the north-west, by afternoon the freezing rain of the morning has turned into a more acceptable steady snowfall. Come late afternoon, we hammer the last nail and pronounce the shelter complete. Satisfied with a job well done and in good spirits, we collect our tools and head to the house. (The sow, by the way, arrived at the farm on schedule the following day. Her newly completed shelter was full of dry bedding, which she apparently took as a sign: she farrowed eight piglets that night.)

In the evening we stoke the fire in the woodstove and relax in our armchairs, I with my whiskey, she with her hot tea and talk over the day. We exchange apologies for any earlier irritability, share laughs as we commiserate about the

miserable weather and acknowledge our relief at having finished the farrowing hut. This talking over the day has served us well for the past 25 years. It is a ritual both morning and evening that gives us a structured chance to discuss joint efforts and individual projects.

The work carried out on a farm – the outbuildings and fences erected, the crops grown and harvested, the livestock raised and sold, birthed and butchered – accretes in layers that eventually become evidence of how a life has been spent. Like a faded trail blaze on an oak, there are telltale signs – additions on a barn or peculiar jogs in a fence – that speak in a coded language a careful observer can decipher. A tight fence line, a solidly built farrowing hut, or an evenly sown field is likely to go unnoticed by anyone but a fellow farmer, who will know what has gone into those tasks and will appreciate their execution when they are done well.

In his 1819 book *The American Gardener*, William Cobbett writes something to the effect that the state of a man's moral life is reflected in the care he shows his gardens and his farm. On my more ambitious days I like to think that the old curmudgeon would grant me membership among the elect or at least allow that I am on the right path. (Although, of course, there are also those dreary winter days when the energy to be a good steward is in as short supply as the daylight.)

Occasionally we host couples who have requested a tour of the farm. Typically, they are starting or planning to start their own farm or homestead. Showing them the hogs is always one of my favourite parts of the visit, and when I do, I inevitably recount that memorable day of ice, snow, wind and the building of the sow shelter. I'll say that how two people work together on such a challenging task will define their future and their farm's success. I'll say that, for us, the work we've done together is the glue that has bound us to the land and to each other – and that satisfaction in working well together and completing a job we are both proud of has naturally followed.

I guess I'm a slow learner: it has taken me all these years to realise that the note above my desk, *Find joy in doing the everyday*, has it backward. As it turns out, I do not need to go looking for joy. If the farm work is done well, whether alone or with companionable help, joy will seek me out.

Today the sow shelter we constructed on that frigid winter's day some 15 years ago continues to serve its purpose. It still hosts the occasional sow and piglets. These days, a family of skunks has found it convenient to den seasonally under the floor. But the time has come that it needs a new workday. A corner post has weakened, and the floor boards have begun to sag. I am sure we will get around to the repairs eventually, squeezing them in among the endless other projects on the farm. This time, hopefully, the work will be done on a sunny spring day.

Solidarity in the Gig Economy

Food-delivery workers across Europe are pushing back against their algorithmic bosses.

BEN WRAY

FOOD DELIVERY: VERY LOW-PAID, zero job security, and, if you do it on a bike, brutal on your body. There's a reason why most 'riders', as they are called, count their time in the food-delivery sector in months, not years.

The industry chews up and spits out workers at a rapid rate, knowing that many of those who stay don't intend to stay long: riding is a stopgap, a means to sustain themselves while they look for something better, and the working conditions are bad.

But a small number of riders have dedicated many years of their lives to delivering pizzas and burgers for an algorithmic boss. They've found something about the job that keeps them coming back for more.

What motivates them to get back on the bike each day, for years on end? I spoke to three such veterans of Europe's food-delivery sector – one in London, one in Berlin, and one in Copenhagen – to find out.

'THE FEAR IS GONE NOW,' Shaf Hussain says in a slightly haunting tone. 'I have had so many accidents and scrapes, it's just not there anymore.'

In London, Hussain was last injured just a month before we meet. He couldn't work for four weeks. Yet despite the bruises and some broken bones, he's back at work on London's slippery, sometimes icy streets the night we meet.

'I love cycling', he says. 'But the main thing about this job for me is the adrenaline. Weaving through rush-hour traffic on my bike at 20 miles an hour, that's the biggest adrenaline high you can get. I need that adrenaline high.'

Hussain first started as a courier all the way back in 2016. There are few riders who manage to stay in the job for so long. They are scythed down from their bikes or motorcycles by poverty, injury, demoralisation. Or – more positively – they find an opportunity for something better.

For Hussain, the physical toll of eight years carrying up to 50 kilos on his back is the single biggest factor pushing him to the exit door.

'I'm 30 now and I feel like I'm 50 years old', he says. 'I've got back issues, neck issues, shoulder issues, legs, palms ... it's getting to the point where I need to quit, or I'll be 35 years old with chronic back pain.'

Hussain, from a working-class family in London's East End, took the typical route into food delivery: discontent with low-paying jobs. In his case, working in the upmarket grocery store Waitrose, on a one-month contract and with a line manager who wouldn't leave him alone. The prospect of a job without a boss to tell you what to do and when to do it made the gig economy sound like an appealing alternative.

In the beginning, it paid reasonably well too. After costs, Hussain could make £500 a week, supplemented with the £400 a week he earned in another contract job doing package delivery, leaving him some money left over for investment.

'I bought Coca-Cola and Microsoft stocks. Not Uber,' he says.

Around 2018, Hussain noticed that the amount he received for each Uber Eats or Deliveroo trip had started to drop. Over the next year, pay rates fell again, and they kept falling year after year. Now, six years on, earnings have collapsed to the point that many riders are working 12 hours a day to survive. Hussain manages to get by only because he lives with his parents and keeps his operating costs as low as possible.

'A lot of the new riders get these big electric bikes that cost about £1,000–£2,000 each year just on maintenance and repairs. I've got a cheap bike with tyres that run for a year each time, and if it gets stolen it doesn't cost me much for a new one.'

But that doesn't mean the falling pay rates don't anger Hussain. He recalls one delivery in London's affluent Soho district, a world away from his home in the mostly impoverished East End. He had delivered steaks worth £80, but his earnings from the delivery amounted to just £3.40.

'The gig economy is zero-rights and zero-protection,' Hussain says. 'All the riders are in the same boat; it's us against the companies.'

Increasingly, riders are turning their anger into action. Before entering the food-delivery sector, Hussain didn't know what a trade union was. Now, he's chair of the courier and logistics branch of the Independent Workers' Union of Great

---

Ben Wray is a journalist specialising in the gig economy. He coordinated The Gig Economy Project, a media network for gig workers in Europe, and has previously written for Wired *and* Jacobin.

Britain. In February 2024, he helped organise a massive strike on Valentine's Day. Across London, riders abandoned their vehicles: instead of picking up deliveries from restaurants, they formed picket lines outside them. The companies profiting from Hussain and his colleagues' hard work sat up and took notice. Uber Eats and Deliveroo doubled or even tripled their regular pay rates, hoping to convince riders to return to work and end the strike.

'I think the strike died out because the riders are not prepared for the long game. They thought

---

'I like to have no boss on my back and to take a break when I want. Plus, I like to be outside, and I enjoy biking.'

---

we could strike a couple of days, and we'd get what we want, but it's not like that. That's why we need a union, because there are people there who are prepared to go the extra mile. But with the strike, you felt that unity', Hussain says. 'You feel that there are people out there who feel what I feel, who are sick and tired of it.'

That stark contrast between the solidarity of the strike and the day-to-day loneliness of delivery work inspired Hussain. In 2016, food delivery was less commonplace in London, and it was easier to get to know other riders. It was also easier to make money, meaning there was more time for chatting and less competitiveness. But all that has changed, he tells me.

'It's so big now that it's mainly people from the same background chilling together; you'll see the Algerians all together, the Indians all together. It's harder to make friends than it was. Sometimes the job feels quite isolating. I just do my thing and then go home.'

Most couriers in London are migrants. Food delivery has low barriers to entry: you don't have to pass a job interview or speak English fluently to do the job. You simply sign up and go. That makes delivery easy to get into, but Hussain says the low pay makes it hard to leave.

'If you come to this country as an immigrant, you want to get to a position of stability, but because the pay is so bad you can't change your situation,' he says. 'You are working 12 hours a day, so you don't have time to try to do anything else. You're stuck in this game.'

Hussain is looking for his way out of the industry, but it's not easy for him either.

'When I had my accident, it derailed my plan to leave the sector because I lost a lot of money,' he says. 'For the past two years I've been saying "I might end it", but it's not happened yet.'

I N BERLIN, 'Mo' has been riding for Lieferando since 2018 (the same company as Just Eat in the United Kingdom and Grubhub in the United States). In contrast to Hussain, he thought delivery work would be a welcome break from organising. Compared with the hyperactivity of student organising he was used to at university, food delivery promised a change of pace.

'I like to have no boss on my back and to take a break when I want. Plus, I like to be outside, and I enjoy biking. I thought I'd do this for two years, take a bit of a break, and maybe do a bit of tenant organising at the same time,' he tells me.

That all changed when Covid-19 hit. As Berlin went into lockdown, demand for food delivery exploded and the number of couriers multiplied. So did the problems they faced, especially around health and safety. Delivery companies seemed interested only in the bottom line, so riders started organising to meet the challenges themselves.

'At first, I didn't get involved because the meetings clashed with my reading group of Karl Marx's *Capital*!' But in the end, Mo tells me, he couldn't resist getting active.

'It was a very small group at first, about 5 to 20 people. We just met in the park.'

The Lieferando Workers' Collective (LWC) was born. At first the group focused on helping workers on an individual, issue-to-issue basis. But most riders would come to the group for help only when they needed it, then go back to work as normal when the problem was solved. Mo felt they weren't building real power for workers in the company. So LWC developed a new strategy.

Unlike most food-delivery platforms, Lieferando riders are legally employees of the company, not self-employed contractors. In Germany, employees have the right to establish a works council that gives them 'co-determination' rights within their company, including a seat on the board and the right to be consulted before significant changes are introduced.

Mo saw the works council as a chance to build real institutional power at Lieferando. When LWC won a majority of seats in the first Lieferando works council election, Mo was one of the riders elected to serve on the new committee. Since then, he's earned a reputation as a highly dedicated representative of his fellow workers.

'I'm a very pragmatic person', he says. 'I don't like to think about things that feel very distant to me. What I get frustrated with a lot is that people talk about the revolution at night, but when you ask them to wake up at nine in the morning and really do the revolution, they don't show up.'

Since then, the works council has won a string of concessions from the company, especially in health and safety. Riders now have the option of carrying deliveries in a basket on their bike rather than porting sometimes heavy containers on their backs – a big reason why chronic back pain is widespread in the industry. Before the works council, the jackets and gloves Lieferando provided were shoddy, the cheapest money could buy, Mo tells me. Now they keep you warm in winter and stop your hands from blistering.

Lieferando riders used to have to complete two one-year fixed term contracts before they had a chance at being made permanent. Now, after the probation period, all riders get permanent contracts – a degree of security in a precarious line of work.

'To achieve those things has been a lot of work; we've had to apply a lot of pressure', Mo says. 'But I can definitely say that it's a better job now than it was when I started at Lieferando. I'm very proud of that.'

The example of the works council in Berlin has inspired delivery workers elsewhere: to date, there are around 20 delivery works councils in cities across Germany. Mo is thinking about what his legacy will be when he finally calls it quits in food delivery.

'I would like it if there would be a second generation who can take over from us at LWC', he says. 'My family gets annoyed and my partner as well because I am not always there for them when I should be. I'm getting old for Lieferando. I always say, "These riders are getting younger and younger", but it's just that I am getting older! Whatever I do next, it will be something to do with organising.'

Rasmus Hjorth learned the hard way about the risks of standing up to the delivery giants. After two years riding around Copenhagen for Wolt, a Finnish platform owned by the US multinational DoorDash, he was abruptly fired. Or in the parlance of the gig economy, his app was 'deactivated.'

'Our partnership is not working', Wolt wrote in a letter to Hjorth. 'We run a business and a partnership that you fundamentally disapprove of. You accept our offer of partnership while taking every opportunity to criticise its foundation, its premise.'

Over his two years at Wolt, Hjorth *did* increasingly disapprove of how the company was run. On paper, individual riders were independent operators, 'partners' contracted by the company to deliver food as a construction firm might be contracted to build an office. In practice though, Hjorth had found that there was no real partnership: riders were dependent on Wolt for their livelihood. He decided that Wolt had to accept its role as an employer. The company should be willing to sit down and talk with unions, like Hjorth's own, 3F, about negotiating a collective agreement with employment contracts for the riders.

Once Hjorth started to get somewhere, building support for a grassroots strike organised by migrant riders in the city, the company decided it was time to cut the cord.

'When I was sacked, it never really occurred to me to stop working as a rider, because I like it,' he says. 'The termination was sad, it hurt my confidence for a while, but it was important for me to keep working in the sector. I have done office jobs before, and I didn't want to do that again.'

Within weeks Hjorth got a job at Just Eat, where he had started his career as a rider in 2020, and where workers do have employment contracts. He dove straight into trade-union organising again.

'I come from a union family,' Hjorth says. 'When I left home, my mum said to me, "Clean your clothes, don't ever ask us for money, and pay your union dues." So the idea of being a trade unionist was always there.'

Hjorth has a special talent for building relationships. Over his five years as a rider, he has built strong links with the migrant communities that make up most of Copenhagen's food-delivery workforce.

'I am a very sociable person, so striking up a conversation with others is not difficult for me,' he says. 'We created a WhatsApp group chat that was the start, and now we have the union club where all the riders meet together regularly. That is really important: you can't do anything without the collaboration of other people. You need to build a community.'

Hjorth's union club started out with just 10 to 15 people. It now has around 420 – a good chunk of the city's riders.

'Now I feel like we are really building that solidarity with one another. We have a union slogan: "You will never ride alone."'

Hjorth is currently the 3F shop steward for Just Eat and was involved in negotiating a new collective agreement in 2023. It increased the length of contracts workers get, increased sick pay, and secured a commitment from the company to pay for sunscreen during the summer. But after five years of cycling and organising, is he not starting to get tired?

'No, I couldn't imagine myself doing anything else, at least not for the moment,' he says. 'When I do stop, I can't see myself in a union job, working in an office. That's not me. If I wasn't connected to the workers, I wouldn't be interested.'

WHILE HUSSAIN, MO, AND HJORTH'S decisions to become riders may have been motivated by a desire to escape the suffocating atmosphere of office jobs or supermarket work, delivery work has become about more than just the job for them. They have each developed a passion for defending their fellow workers – and all have developed skills in organising workers that they'll take with them to whatever they do next.

These experiences also show something else: food delivery isn't necessarily doomed to always be a bad job. Even in the gig economy, it's possible for workers to band together, connect with one another, and make a change. Even if that change is very small or superficial to begin with, it's the experience of fighting for your rights alongside others that fosters community and dignity at work. And who knows, if enough Hussains, Mos, and Hjorths leave their mark on the industry, maybe one day work as a rider won't be a last resort or a temporary gig, and to be a veteran of the food-delivery sector will no longer be something out of the ordinary.

Thomas Cole, *The Garden of Eden*, oil on canvas, 1828.

The Divine Rhythm of Work and Sabbath

The story of labour begins in Eden – and its ending is still to come.

ALASTAIR ROBERTS

Holy Scripture begins with a working week. Over the course of seven days, the Lord brings the creation into being, fashions its structures, fills its realms with life, and delegates aspects of its rule to appointed agents. Each successive day is numbered and punctuated with the refrain 'and there was evening and there was morning …' and divine acts of assessment of his creations, both severally and collectively, are scattered throughout the account: 'And God saw that it was good.'

Within the stable rhythm of the creation days, the creative work of God is richly varied in its form and its objects. God speaks and brings light into being; he separates light from darkness; he assesses his creation; he names his creatures; he makes an expanse; he charges and enlivens the earth to bring forth vegetation; he appoints sun, moon, and stars to be for signs and for seasons in the heavens; he blesses the fish and birds with fruitfulness and empowers them to multiply and fill the seas and earth; he creates humankind. And on the seventh day he rests, blessing and sanctifying the day.

The reader of Genesis might be surprised that an almighty God did not bring the entire creation into existence in a single instant. Yet a key dimension of God's work of creation is setting up the continued rhythms, orders, and patterns of

> The pattern of labour and rest is fundamentally divine; in our work, we continue a pattern established in God's own creative work.

the creation. Within his working week in creation God sets the pattern for human labour. The pattern of the day (evening and morning) and the pattern of the week (six days of labour, one day of rest) do not result from some limitation on God's part, but from God's purpose to set the pattern for his creatures' labour and to dignify that labour by establishing a continuity between his own creation work and creaturely sub-creation.

On the sixth day, God creates humankind in his image and likeness, blessing them and commissioning them: 'Be fruitful and multiply and fill the earth and subdue it, and have dominion over the fish of the sea and over the birds of the heavens and over every living thing that moves on the earth.' Humanity's task continues God's own creation, filling the realms that God established, extending and elaborating good order within the creation, and exercising beneficent rule over its creatures. Humankind both had to rule over and to share the creation with other creatures.

In Genesis 2, the creation is described as incompletely ordered, filled, and ruled: 'when no bush of the field was yet in the land and no small plant of the field had yet sprung up – for the Lord God had not caused it to rain on the land, and there was no man to work the ground.' The original creation is good, yet much remains to be done. God creates, commissions, empowers, and equips humanity to complete what he has started; we are a means of his continued creation and providence.

The man was created in the wilderness, and then God created the garden. Presumably the man witnessed God's formation of the garden: this is what it looks like to tame, order, and glorify the wilderness. The garden, a beautiful, bounded, and ordered realm, was a model, training ground, staging area and orienting heart for humanity's labour. Placed in the garden, the man was given the task of serving and guarding it, defending its bounded order and encouraging its flourishing. As several scholars have observed, the task given to Adam in the garden is the same as that given to the Levites relative to the tabernacle.

Downstream from the garden lay other lands; their treasures are described in the account – the Pishon flowed around Havilah, a land of gold and precious stones. Having learned the ropes in the garden, humanity, the reader presumes, would need to venture out and start to tame the wider world, the task for which we originally were created. The garden was also an elevated sanctuary, a realm where God and man enjoyed fellowship. There was a centrifugal impulse, by which man would be propelled out from the garden to the four corners of the earth (suggested by the four rivers). There was also a centripetal impulse, by which humanity would always return to the garden sanctuary, glorifying it with the treasures of the creation.

Adam, alone in the garden, was completely

Alastair Roberts teaches for both the Theopolis Institute and the Davenant Institute. He and his wife, Plough *editor Susannah Black Roberts, split their time between New York City and the United Kingdom.*

insufficient for the task that lay before him. He lacked the capacity to be fruitful, multiply and to fill the earth. He needed a fitting counterpart by his side, not chiefly for companionship to address his personal loneliness, but for effective performance of his God-given commission. Before creating a counterpart for Adam, however, God gave the man the task of naming the animals. While God had named some of his creatures on the first three days, the creatures of the later days remained unnamed. Like a father training his son in the family business, God taught Adam the business of ordering and understanding creation through speech. Work, then, is not just physical and creative: it is intellectual as well. There is an implication that Adam, in his naming, was making what might be judgement calls: discerning the nature of the creatures he was naming. Man's labour is thus continuous with, and established by God's labour.

Although he successfully named the animals, Adam was unsuccessful in finding a suitable counterpart. When Adam awoke to see the woman God fashioned from the rib he took from him, he greeted her with delight, recognising not merely a fitting counterpart but a companion in relation to whom he could arrive at a new self-knowledge: 'This at last is bone of my bones and flesh of my flesh; she shall be called Woman, because she was taken out of Man.' He could recognise her in part because his work of naming had prepared him to do so: the work of naming is thus also a work of love.

A rich account of human work is already implicit within the first two chapters of Holy Scripture. The pattern of labour and rest is fundamentally divine; in our work, we continue a pattern established in God's own creative work. Besides following a pattern of divine work, human work continues what began in divine work, further filling, ordering, naming, taming, and glorifying creation. Human labour is a participation in divine labour, in God's ordering of, provision for, ruling over, and glorifying of his creation. Humankind is created for the purpose of labour – 'to work the ground' – and blessed and commissioned for the task – 'Be fruitful and multiply.' That fruitfulness and multiplication entails another kind of work: the labour of women in childbirth, contextualised as central to the other kinds of work that men and women do. Created in the image and likeness of God, humankind has a capacity for transforming creative activity in the world that no other earthly creature possesses. It is difficult to imagine a firmer basis for the dignity of work than that offered in Genesis 1 and 2.

It is in his work that man takes an active interest in and responsibility for the creation and fellow creatures; through work he can deepen and enrich his relationship with the ground from which he was first formed. God created man to make a divinely

Thomas Cole, *The Garden of Eden* (detail).

desired mark upon the world, so that his work would be fruitful, effective and good. Through labour, man will mature in skill, understanding, wisdom and agency. In the garden, man is offered a model and training for his task, the connection between his work and God's work further underlined. The realm of the garden is to be maintained by the wisdom and skill of the man and caring for it trains him in skills by which he would later fashion such realms of his own. Fellow-labour is also a primary basis of human fellowship: the man and the woman are created in a shoulder-to-shoulder relationship, not merely a face-to-face one. Together, they will be fruitful and multiply, labour, make a world and make a home – world and home are places both of work and of rest.

Beyond the marriage relationship, collaborative labour binds people together and establishes contexts of belonging, mutual dependence, common concern and common good. While talk of 'the economy' or 'the market' may often function as unhelpful abstractions, they can relate to the 'commonwealth' formed by the multifaceted entanglement and interdependence of the labour and interests of many people in some realm. Work is the form that participation in a larger society can take.

M AN'S WORK WAS SUPPOSED to flow out of and back into fellowship with God: it was ordered out from and into the sanctuary. However, after humanity's rebellion in the Fall, human labour went awry, adopting a different character. Alienated from God, human labour lost its primary orientation to communion, becoming acquisitive, driven by a desire for material possessions, power and status. Capacities that were created for beneficent rule were twisted to the ends of domination over others, and labour became entangled with systems of bondage. Mutual recognition, companionship, and belonging through fellow labour curdled into rivalry and division. Work once blessed with fruitfulness was reduced to frustration and futility. Labour degraded into unrelenting toil. The earth no longer readily answered to the efforts of the man and now, alienated from the Giver of Life, man's labours were constantly slipping down into the pitiless maw of death. The labour of women in childbirth became hedged about with the risk of death, for mother and

baby alike. The book of Ecclesiastes, which meditates upon the condition of man in a world under the power of death, describes how man's greatest works are washed away and forgotten beneath the advancing tides of time.

At the heart of the biblical story of the Exodus is the theme of labour. Egypt is described as 'the house of slavery' and not merely on account of the children of Israel's reduced condition within it: the whole land and its population are characterised by a cruel distortion of labour. The children of Israel were afflicted and placed under bondage. In place of the creational dignity, fruitfulness, and fellowship of labour, and its ordering

Thomas Cole, *The Course of Empire: The Arcadian or Pastoral State*, oil on canvas, 1834.

around fellowship with God, they experienced the mastery of merciless tyrants, continuous and unforgiving toil, alienation from the fruits of their work and the enervation of their peoplehood and spirit under crushing burdens.

To many readers it might feel that the kinetic narrative of the book of Exodus loses its steam somewhere around the halfway mark, its energy petering out in a tedious morass of obscure case laws, instructions for the tabernacle and its furniture and a lengthy account of the process of its construction. Yet, if the first half of the book described the deliverance of the children of Israel from oppression in Egypt, the second half establishes the laws and institutions by which they might enjoy continued freedom. In the provision of the manna in chapter 16, the people were already being prepared for a new form of life. Their former life had been one of daily toil without rest, struggling to find the means of survival. Now their daily bread was provided by God and all had a sufficient amount, one omer. As it could not be accumulated, they had to learn a grateful and trusting dependence upon God's provision. On the sixth day enough was provided for two days and, on the seventh, they were charged to rest. Sabbath rest was a revolutionary transformation of the manner of life to which they had been accustomed.

In the Ten Commandments in Exodus 20, the law of the Sabbath was given its rationale in God's own rest after the six days of creation: in its practice, a former slave people were called to follow God's own pattern of labour and to liberate others in their turn. As the principle of Sabbath was expounded and expanded upon in the rest of the Pentateuch, it was related to civil legislation concerning the liberation of slaves and provision for the poor. The weekly Sabbath was also the seed of a calendrical principle that was elaborated into a festal year with an annual cycle of seven festivals, seven days of rest, two seven-day feasts, and the Feast of Weeks or Pentecost as a Sabbath of Sabbaths, seven sevens from the Feast of Firstfruits (where the omer presented to the Lord recalled the people to the lesson of divine provision of the manna). Expanded further, it was expressed in a sabbatical year and the year of Jubilee (after seven sets of seven years).

These feasts and years grounded Israel's life in the rest freely granted by the Lord. They memorialised and occasioned thanksgiving for his deliverance and provision and prayer for its continuation. In celebrating them, Israel enjoyed the fruits of their labours and shared them with others, especially the poor, the stranger, and the Levite. They were times of assembly, community, and festivity, ordering Israel's labour to thanksgiving, enjoyment of God's good gifts and liberality to others. Due to the division of labour, societies are typically stratified and their members separated by their diverse economic activities; the feast was

Thomas Cole, *The Course of Empire: The Arcadian or Pastoral State* (detail).

a reassertion of commonality, mutual interest, and mutual recognition, tempering tendencies towards the alienation of classes both from each other and from a greater shared peoplehood.

The Sabbath principle was not exclusive to free Israelites: Israelites were charged to give rest to their servants, animals and all within their households. Indeed, in the seventh year, the rest was explicitly extended to the land itself, which was to lie fallow. Likewise, in connection with the Feast of Weeks and the year of Jubilee, God's concern that no Israelite be alienated from his gift of the land is demonstrated: even the poorest must be allowed to glean and all ancestral property must be restored to its original owners in the 50th year.

The tabernacle, the construction of which is the focus of the second half of Exodus, is akin to a Sabbath *place*, a realm of God's rest amidst his liberated people. The various feasts grounded in the Sabbath are ordered around the reality of the tabernacle as the site of festal gathering and of fellowship with God, and the presentation of gifts. The plan for the tabernacle and its furniture in Exodus 25–31 is delivered in two cycles of seven sections, paralleled to the days of creation: fittingly the instructions conclude with the law of the Sabbath as the great sign of the covenant. The book of Exodus begins with the children of Israel building store cities for the Pharaoh and it ends with Spirit-empowered Israelite artisans constructing a tent palace for God to dwell in their midst.

THE DAILY CYCLE OF WORK and rest, the weekly cycle of six days of labour followed by the Sabbath, the annual cycle of feasts and the larger cycle of sabbatical years both punctuated and variegated Israel's time. Time was meaningfully articulated, structured, ordered to new ends and differentiated in its character. Through such an articulation of time, Israel was granted the possibility of transcending a flat quotidian grind. Time was 'redeemed', related to the fundamental time of creation in the continued recapitulation of the first week of God's labour, to the times of redemption in the memorial feasts, and to the awaited consummation through the eschatological import of such celebrations. In such a manner, work could be bounded, differentiated from rest and leisure, flowing from a higher source and being ordered towards a higher end. Bitter toil and cruel bondage could become good work and sacred service.

Through sabbatical times and the tabernacle as the sabbatical place, the fallenness of the time of Israel's bondage was overcome and its time and its labours were liberated. The goods of labour that were compromised or lost in the Fall and the evils introduced into humanity's experience of work were addressed. Sabbath presented work with an *end*, being both a cessation of otherwise unre-

---

Sabbath presented work with an *end*, being both a cessation of toil and a purpose: an orientation to something greater that upholds its goodness.

---

lenting toil and a purpose: an orientation of work to something greater that upholds its goodness.

By placing the Lord's rest at the heart of Israel, the entire realm of man's times and labours was reordered. The people of Israel were called to present themselves before the Lord, along with the fruit of their labours. They were to celebrate before the Lord with the fruit of their labours, enjoying fellowship with the Lord and with each other. Structures of bondage, alienation and separation were to be loosened as people assembled before the God who gave rest to all his people. Israel's times of festal assembly corresponded with times of harvest and ingathering, relating their labours to dependence upon and thanksgiving for God's good gifts. In the Ark of the Covenant, within the Holy of Holies, was a measure of the manna that God had given – the bread from heaven, the harvest for which the Israelites had not laboured, a reminder of the gratuitous nature of God's way with them, even as their own labour was made holy. It is God who gives us our daily bread, as he gave it to Israel in the desert.

The liberating principle of Sabbath remains for Christians, although its root meaning may now be differently conjugated. We still cease from our labours and practice sacred rest. We still assemble to celebrate together, to memorialise the deliverances of God and await the consummation of all things. We still present ourselves as labourers and present the fruits of our labours to God. We still enjoy communion with God amidst our labours. We do not have Israel's tabernacle or the Garden of Eden, but we still have sanctuaries of worship to which we ascend, relating our downstream activity in the wider world to the central spring of life before the face of God among his people.

Through such practices, our labour can be redeemed, discovering its true end. Regularly returning to God's rest and anticipating the greater rest that awaits us, our labour is dignified and elevated. Jobs can become *vocations*. As the apostle Paul taught in Ephesians 6:5–8, when done in the service of Christ, even the most menial and thankless toil can be rendered honourable and fruitful, receiving the recognition and approbation of our Lord. As a body of many members, each exercising its own distinctive gifts for the good of the whole, the church is a *communion* of spirited labour.

And at the heart of the church's life is God's taking of our gifts of bread and wine – fruits and tokens of our labour – and returning them to us as the gift of his Son, the true bread that came down from heaven, his making of them into the perfect offering that we could never have made of ourselves: the offering that atones, the bread that gives everlasting life. The futility of fallen labour is also overcome in Christ, as our work for God's kingdom is now assured of final fruitfulness. As 1 Corinthians 15:58 charges us, 'Therefore, my beloved brothers, be steadfast, immovable, always abounding in the work of the Lord, knowing that in the Lord your labour is not in vain.'

We still live in a fallen world, with all its frustration, toil, and bondage. Yet as we and our labours are brought into the life of the church, we have a promissory reality of a world beyond the dominion of death and can experience something of humanity's restoration in the good work for which we were first created.

The Book of Revelation concludes with images that recall the opening chapters of Genesis. In a book replete with significant sevens, the coming of God's great and final rest is declared. The final vision is of a great city descending out of heaven, like a bride prepared for her husband. Hearers might be excused for feeling a sense of déjà vu: it describes a nuptial scene in a garden city, with a river of the water of life flowing out, flanked by the tree of life. It is a return to Eden, but an Eden glorified with the treasures of the world, all the good work and works that all peoples have ever done caught up in this new regime and made permanent, none of them lost. In this Eden the vocation of man to be fruitful, multiply, fill the earth, subdue it and exercise dominion over its creatures has been achieved, the wonderful fruits of that labour are enjoyed and all humanity knows communion with God and each other.

The Work of the Poet

Poetry makes us more fit to inhabit reality.

CHRISTIAN WIMAN

Plough: You've written more than a handful of books of poetry. What is the work of the poet?

Christian Wiman: That depends on the poet. But if there's a unifying task it is to enable and advance consciousness. R P Blackmur once wrote of John Berryman's metaphors that they 'enlarged the scope of available reality.' The observation can be generalised: a true poem makes reality more available to us, and makes us more fit to inhabit it. I also believe, with everything in me, that poetry is a 'foretaste of truth', as Anna Kamienska wrote: 'It is the vestibule of faith.' A deep response to the mysterious life of poetry, even secular poetry, can make an even deeper response to life itself seem suddenly tenable.

What does a day of work look like when you are writing poetry?

Chaos. I move around, mutter, curse, stare at the sky for an hour, occasionally stop all this to hastily scribble a flurry of words down (which I often have a hard time reading later). But then sometimes – the best times – it's quite swift and 40 years of it, I find the experience more rather than less comprehensible. I do believe God is in it, both the source and the aim.

What nourishes your capacities as a poet?

Time and silence. As I've written before, I find I can write prose in just about any circumstance, but poetry requires a lot of empty space and time to emerge. Which is why I pretty much never write a poem when I am teaching. Reading, too, can be very generative. Sometimes someone else's phrases seem to cast me out of their words and into my own. That, too, is very mysterious to me and utterly unpredictable.

Who are the poets and writers who have inspired you in your work as a poet?

Too many to name. But the first living poet I responded to was Seamus Heaney, whose work remains deeply important to me. Wordsworth and Herbert are abiding presences. Among contemporaries, there is my wife, Danielle Chapman, who not only reads everything I write but whose words (written and spoken) often trigger my imagination in saving ways. I would also mention the work of Atsuro Riley, which is marked by a true sacramental imagination and which I return to regularly for consolation and inspiration.

This interview was conducted by Joy Clarkson on 24 January 2025. Read a new poem by Christian Wiman on the next page.

Yulia Brodskaya, *Jungle Bird*, paper quilling, 2009.

The Eye

Among the monks was one who kept apart.
A gifted pray-er, they said of him,
who sensed my faith was mostly faith in art.
A man of fluent, fasted absences
that from his tongue would come as scalding psalms,
then yearlong silences of solid God.
A keeper of the ancient ways, they said,
(which I took to mean insane) who gleaned
between the hapless captive and the called;
and that no richer privilege could befall
a muddled soul than to receive his blessing.
For seven weeks he never met my eyes.
For seven itchy, unctuous, dyspeptic
and penitential weeks he kept me guessing
where he'd be, or if the long sighs
at Mass or matins were, somehow, for me.
How could he not become my avatar
of all things holy and opaque,
with his tonsured top and mortared neck,
his gravid aspect and air of scar,
but buoyant, too, as a battleship is buoyant,
with cello legs and a cello's walk;
and a raucous root-vegetable face
out of Bruegel or Bosch.

Oh—and the eye that had offended—
or so I told myself—replaced
with one of weirdly faceted glass
that even in the candled chapel flashed
a lively dialogue with light.
Some spoke of healings from his hands.
Two brothers swore they saw him levitate.
But all I saw was somber truculence,
lord so-and-so and la-di-da (though once
he hawked an egg of snot into the grate).
Unlikely—that's the word that came to mind,
like a concupiscent porcupine
(how proud I was of that one line!).
Still, I clung to what they claimed
and when the time for leaving came
sensed, rightly, that the time was mine.
He strode right up as if he knew me
and looking not so much at as through me
—as if I were a skull occluding sky—
leaned in close and whispered: *Why?*
And walked away.

I tried to laugh but only choked.
I tried to speak but had no voice.
The other monks all fawned and spoke
as if in fact some scathing grace
had driven me to my knees
and a self not mine had uttered *Please*
not knowing but knowing not to ask
if I was asking for fulfillment or release.
No. Just this pious pumpkin with his why.
Just this mild and unavailing I.
Just this low, mortar, mop-water void of sky.
I stumbled out. They closed the gate.
I didn't know if I should weep or celebrate
but felt one clear imperative: do not forget.
I vowed a higher kind of have,
a something more than memory
fusing fact and faith, world and mind
so each particular might shine
until the whole disclosed its key.

But no: the very first step I took
took something from me—that communal chant
that seemed so sad—and away was all I had.
Those days of prayer and what I'd begged,
that pumpkin monk with his cello legs
(who in truth I have embellished),
the storm-colored cassocks and tempest beards
all vanished, everything except that *why*.
That's real. Seared.
Oh—and the weird sight of his unseeing eye.

CHRISTIAN WIMAN

Yulia Brodskaya, *Melting*, paper quilling, 2015.

The Apurímac Clinic

A truck brings medical care to remote Quechua communities in Peru.

A photo essay by Maria Novella De Luca
with text by Monica Pelliccia and Alice Pistolesi

Survival can be complex in the south-central peaks of the Peruvian mountains, 4,000 metres above sea level, and when medical treatment is required it is more complex still. But for over a decade, an NGO run by an Augustinian foreign mission – the Apurímac ETS – has brought doctors into the Andes to provide medical care for indigenous Quechua communities. Difficult to access due to poor roads, the Apurímac region is one of the most impoverished in the country. Cardiovascular and chronic respiratory diseases, cancer and diabetes are leading causes of death in the region and these health problems are often compounded by poor hygiene and nutrition, a subsistence economy and low literacy.

In 2024, the NGO carried out five health campaigns in 15 villages, providing medical care to more than 3,000 people. Each team uses a truck fitted with a specialised mobile unit, a laboratory and a pharmacy. 'In almost ten years of activity, we've encountered a lot of chronic diseases linked to the high-altitude living conditions, such as thermal shock and dermatitis caused by the sun,' explains Vittorio Villa, director of Apurímac ETS.

'Also, dental disease and diabetes are common, as people tend to consume very sugary foods and drinks. Anaemia and other nutritional diseases are also prevalent, linked to a poor diet consisting almost exclusively of chicken, rice, and potatoes.'

The medical support does not end with the truck visits. In the past few years, the NGO has introduced telemedicine in 21 communities, providing equipment and training to local nurses, laboratory technicians and doctors.

The Apurímac ETS mobile clinic travels to a mountain village (above) where medical care is provided for indigenous Quechua communities (opposite).

Yessly with her mother and grandmother.

Baby Yessly

Baby Yessly, nine months old, has been diagnosed with microcephaly. Her mother, Yanina, age 19, and her grandmother arrived on foot and approached the truck asking for medical assistance.

Appropriate therapy, however, is only available at the hospital in the nearby city of Cusco. Yanina was abandoned by her husband and is currently living with her parents who are helping her as well as coping with many difficulties of their own. As the family was unable to afford the trip to the city, the NGO's medical staff took Yessly and Yanina to Cusco, where the baby will receive therapy to improve mobility in her legs and hands and strengthen her head posture. 'We never leave our patients alone,' explains a medical staffer travelling on the truck, 'They are people who have never been to the city and feel lost and afraid there. So from the first home visit to the meetings with specialists, there will always be someone with them to help them communicate with the doctors, and to take care of their food and any other needs they may have.'

Edison

Edison is 12 years old and has Noonan syndrome, a genetic condition characterised by short stature, facial dysmorphism, muscle contractures, and cardiomyopathy. His gait, speech and language skills are severely affected, and he has low self-esteem. His father, who brought him to the healthcare team, only speaks Quechua, so his sister interprets into Spanish for the doctors. 'Edison is so young; he has many years ahead. He needs support and physical therapy,' explains a health worker. 'He struggles with some of the simplest movements.' The team hopes to give him more self-confidence with physical therapy and neurological treatments.

Edison with his father and sister.

Alizon Brenda (above, left) and Edith Giovanna Vellegas Alfaro (opposite, bottom left).

Edith Giovanna Villegas Alfaro

Edith Giovanna Villegas Alfaro and her daughter Alizon Brenda are part of the caravan's medical staff. Edith, 55, lives in Abancay City, a town in the Apurímac region and works as a laboratory technician in the Metropolitan Health Centre. Edith has already carried out ten health campaigns in Quechua communities with the NGO. 'I love going on the campaigns because I can see the changes in the communities over the years,' she says. 'What I like most is to work in tranquillity: out here, we forget the city and can totally dedicate ourselves to the patients who need us the most.'

---

*Monica Pelliccia is an Italian freelance multimedia journalist who covers environmental and social issues such as climate change, indigenous peoples' rights, food security, and agroecology. **Alice Pistolesi** is an Italian journalist whose work focuses on the conditions of oppressed populations and on environmentalist and feminist protest movements. **Maria Novella De Luca** is a photojournalist who has worked with various press agencies and national newspapers. She currently collaborates with NGOs to create social and travel documentary photos and videos.*

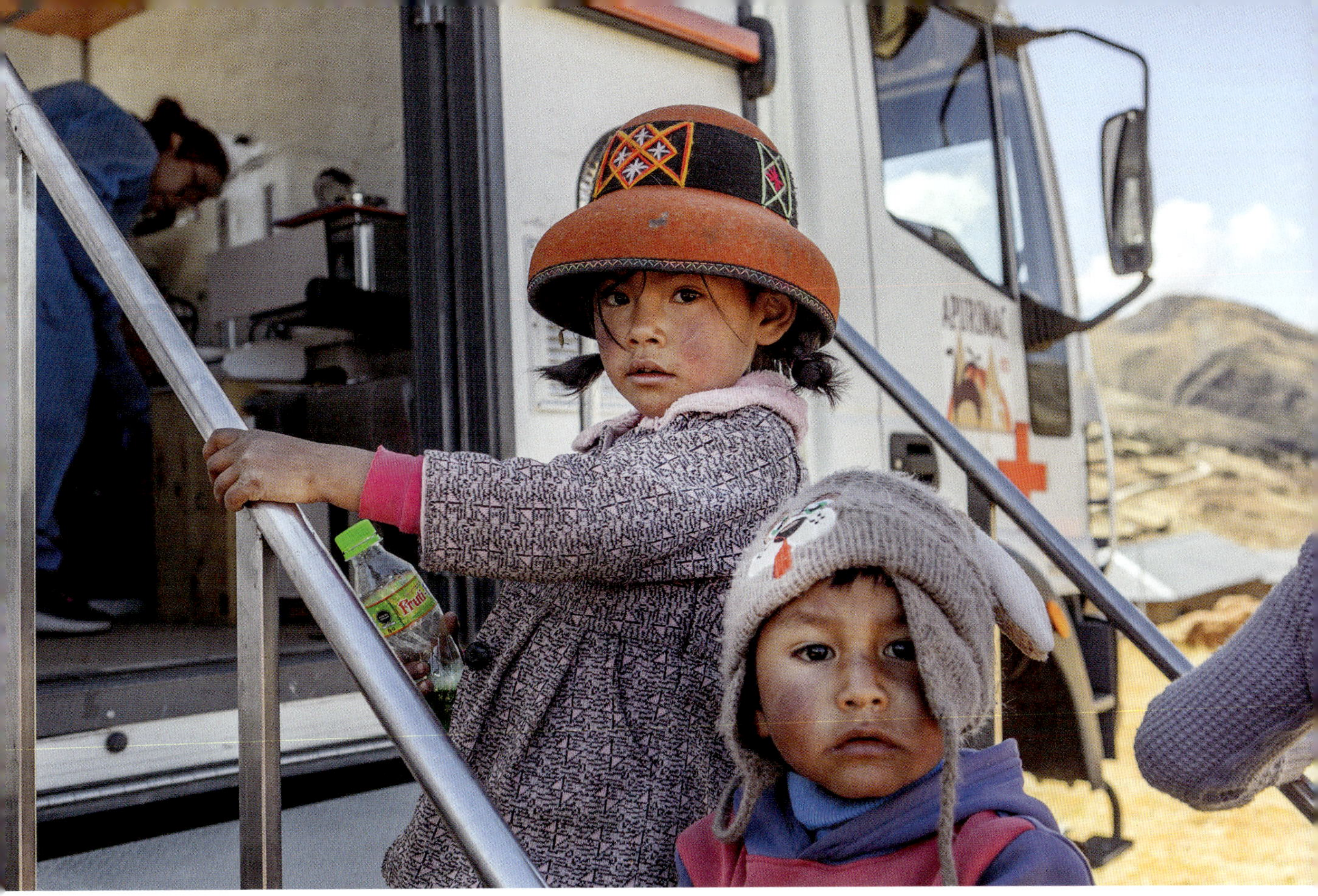

PROHIBIDO EL
INGRESO DE
PERSONAS NO
AUTORIZADAS

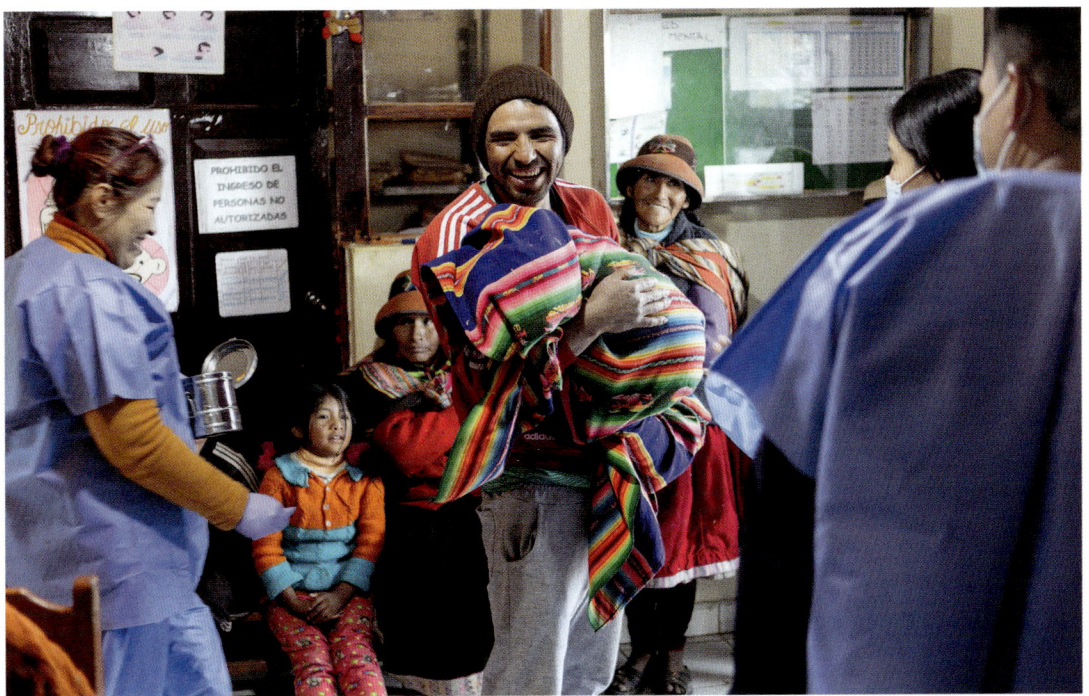

REFLECTION

STEPHANIE SALDAÑA

The Solace of the Cross

In a Holy Land wracked by violence, remembering the crucifixion brings comfort.

For many years, I have believed that as Christians we must read the Gospels, as we must read our own lives, in the light of the resurrection. We are called to return to every moment in the life of Jesus, no matter how small: his walks along the shore of the Sea of Galilee, the bread he broke amongst friends, his prayers whispered beneath the olive trees – and see within them a hidden hope, waiting to be revealed. That is what it means to find the joy hidden among ordinary things. That knowledge of resurrection has served as my source of strength in many times of difficulty.

Yet it is only now, after so many years of living in proximity to war, violence and displacement, that I have come to believe that we might also learn to read the gospels and so our own lives, in the light of the crucifixion. This also is a source of strength.

We can return to every moment in the ministry of Jesus – the Sermon on the Mount, the calming of the storm – carrying within our hearts the certainty of Jesus, crucified. And this knowledge will give us not only pain, but also solace and the fortitude to live.

Yes, it is only in these most difficult years that I have come to know the solace of the cross, the solace of God who never stops loving us. It is in the moments of exhaustion, on more occasions than I can count, that I have remembered Jesus in his last moments, hung in agony, with his arms outstretched and nailed to wooden beams. In this moment he is only love. Deeply himself. Jesus, fully human and fully divine, who sees us.

That is the Jesus I have come to seek, a man of absolute tenderness. I have watched him, in his last hours, quietly making choices. Attentive, present, steady, a witness to the constancy of love.

He notices everyone around him. Even as he suffers and dies, he keeps offering his life in love. Jesus on the cross, who forgives those who

Father Nevin Ford, OFM, *Stations of the Cross No 5*, mosaic at the Old Mission Santa Barbara, California, ca. 1960.

crucified him, calling out: 'Forgive them Father, for they know not what they do.' Not only remembering them, but loving them, watching out for them.

Jesus, who speaks tenderly to the thief hanging beside him: 'Truly, I tell you, today you will be with me in Paradise.' And in doing so not only hears him, but accompanies him, offering encouragement in his greatest hour of agony.

Jesus, who says to John: 'Behold your mother.' And to his mother: 'Here is your son.'

Jesus, who prays the psalms.

Jesus, who cries out. Who is thirsty.

Jesus, who says simply: 'Into your hands I commend my spirit.'

It is this Jesus on the cross who comes to me in these dark times. All compassion. All goodness. Jesus, who in his torment remains fully available, connected. Who reads the hearts of those around him, as he reads ours.

Starting from there, I can return and re-read the Gospels in a new way, for I know that his teachings, even the most difficult ones, are not only true in quiet times. For isn't it easy to speak of hunger when we have food, of forgiveness when no one has wounded us? But Jesus teaches everything again by living it on the cross, simply in being himself, in that place, at that hour.

Love your enemy. Do good to those who hate you.

Bless those who curse you. Pray for those who abuse you.

Turn the other cheek. Love your neighbour as yourself.

Do good to others as you would have them do unto you.

His words remain true. And in being true, they are not only solace. They are also miracle.

Truly, this was the son of God.

Watching him, I know that this is how I want to attempt to live in the world, strengthened with the love of God. Carrying the knowledge that cruelty and violence have lost their power. Even in wartime. Even if everything else should be destroyed. I want to remember that it is possible to still be kind. It is possible to love. It is possible to forgive. It is possible to remain present to the needs of others.

And so, knowing this solace of the cross, the urge comes to live in the world with a little bit more compassion. To offer to lift someone else's heavy bags. To open a door. To bandage a wound. To smile. To call someone by name. To place one's head at the foot of a child's bed after an exhausting day, and sing a lullaby. The urge comes to love not only in response to the violence of the world, but as an end in and of itself. Because that is God loving with us and in us. And I can notice those around me, living this kindness against gravity, day after day, largely unnoticed, and I can recognise the miracle in it.

This is my prayer, that in carrying the solace of the crucifixion, it might be possible to move in the world with a little less fear. The freedom of the cross is in this – that God has made it possible to love, even in the face of violence and war and hatred, and death itself. In this knowledge, darkness, at least for a moment, loses its power, for it cannot destroy what is dearest to us. What is true is true and will always be true.

So we return to the beginning of the Gospels and read the words again in the light of the cross, strengthened in trust that it will guide us.

Forgive, and you will be forgiven
   (And this is true, even on the cross)
Give and it will be given to you
   (And this is true, even on the cross)
Do not worry about your life
   (And this is true, even on the cross)
Love one another, as I have loved you.

Stephanie Saldaña is the author, most recently, of What We Remember Will Be Saved: A Story of Refugees and the Things They Carry *(Broadleaf Books, 2023). She lives in the Holy Land with her family.*

The Revival of the Cloister

Why are so many young Catholic women becoming cloistered nuns?

SHIRA TELUSHKIN

When Sister Christiana entered the Poor Clare Colettine monastery in Alexandria, Virginia, USA in 1993, her parents were concerned. The Poor Clares have not worn shoes since 1406, the year their 1211 order was reformed, not even socks. They wake every day at half past midnight to pray matins, and then again at 5am for lauds. In addition to chastity, obedience, and poverty, they vow to stay enclosed within the monastery walls for the rest of their lives.

'Does this mean she will not be able to come to me on my deathbed?' her father had asked the Mother Abbess, after learning the strict rules of enclosure. She would not. Poor Clares never leave the monastery once they've taken their perpetual vows, not even for funerals. The Abbess was reassuring. *When you are on your deathbed, every nun here will be praying for you.*

The words of the Mother Abbess brought comfort.

'It changed his perspective, to envision a whole monastery praying for him,' Sister Christiana said in a recent phone interview. 'It flips what you're losing to what you are gaining.'

Later, her father would tell her that he understood: nuns magnify God's power in the world, he said, by giving themselves completely to him in prayer, enabling God to do more for more people.

It was a sentiment wholly out of vogue in the 1990s, but one that has found surprising resonance among a new generation of Catholic women.

Nearly every story about American Catholic nuns begins with a few statistics: in 1966, there were 181,421 Catholic women religious in the United States, as nuns and sisters are called. (Well, technically, only the cloistered and contemplative are nuns, while active women religious are sisters, but the terms are often used interchangeably.) In 2006, there were 67,000. In 2017, there were 45,605. Even considering the sharp, unprecedented growth of monastic life in the 1940s and 1950s, that's a reduction of over 75 percent.

> *'I figured if I was going do something crazy for our Lord I may as well go all in.'*
> —Sister Rosalie Agnes

The story that follows these statistics is usually simple: our modern, secular age has no ear for monastic callings. The life of a cloistered nun, with her endless prayers and heavy woollen headdress, is squarely in the past, and the allure of being an active sister, who ran hospitals and schools and fought for civil rights, belongs to a time when women had few other opportunities to work outside the home. Today, women who want to serve the world can be social workers, nurses, teachers, or directors of non-profits, all without the restrictions of consecrated life. The nun has outlived her purpose.

But this story overlooks a far more interesting development: not all religious orders are losing numbers, and not all at the same rate. In the past 15 years, the most traditional, cloistered orders have found themselves awash in interest. New monasteries are being built; more land is being bought. Ancient forms of religious life, such as those for canonical hermits and consecrated virgins, are once more on the rise. Though it is true that most sisters today are active, the orders attracting younger members are contemplative: they pray the full office, wear traditional habits, and seek lives of worship and devotion away from the world, renouncing family, comfort and travel – the type of monasticism that has existed in the church for 2,000 years.

'It's radical, and we know it is radical. When young women want to embrace the contemplative life nowadays, they're looking for *radical* change', Sister Bernadette, 26, told me on a chilly day in late November as we walked the grounds of her Carmelite monastery in Fairfield, Pennsylvania, USA. (To honour their hidden life, the Fairfield Carmelites asked me to use pseudonyms.) 'When I decided I wanted to be a nun, it was so that I could learn how to love Jesus the best, and the best place to do that is obviously a Carmelite monastery, because they're the most intense.'

The monastery in Fairfield is certainly intense. It was established in 2018 on undeveloped land; its eight sisters' goal is to live without electricity or running water. Everything has been built from the ground up. The oratory is heated with metal air ducts connected to a Roman-style hypocaust that burns under heat-retaining granite stones. Nuns get water via hand pumps connected to filtered cisterns of water. Until they could get a roof on the barn, everyone slept in trailers. The community has grown rapidly and has established two new monasteries to meet demand. Every year, more women arrive, drawn specifically by the construction site, the promise of radical devotion, and the sacrifices it requires.

'I figured if I was going do something crazy for our Lord I may as well go all in,' said Sister Rosalie Agnes, 23, who arrived at Fairfield in 2020.

Shira Telushkin is a writer living in Brooklyn. She teaches religion reporting at the Craig Newmark Journalism school at CUNY. Her first book, How to Forsake the World, *will be published by HarperCollins this year.*

A former hairdresser from North Carolina, her first night involved hours of laying brick in the dark with other sisters, building the foundation for what will eventually be the refectory. 'So why not have no running water, no electricity, living in a stone building, sleeping on straw. I wanted the real thing, as real as I could possibly get in this society.'

This desire for something real is pervasive among the nearly two dozen nuns I interviewed across religious orders. They don't want something easy, catered to their needs; every algorithm they've encountered has done the same. They want to live in a world shaped by something higher than their own instincts and interests. The rigours of cloistered life – waking at 5am, regular fasting, forgoing novels and trips to the beach and chats with friends – are exciting, when they promise a purposeful life in return.

It is hard to imagine what it is like to be cloistered, to see no people except fellow sisters. The Carmelite nuns in Fairfield see family only four days a year, always from behind a double-grille wall. They take communion through a wooden

turn and give confession through a grate opening at their ankles. The sisters I meet are externs, formerly cloistered nuns now tasked to greet visitors and organise the sacristy for daily mass, requiring they leave the boundaries of the enclosure. For this degree of worldly access, they sleep, eat, and pray separately from the fully cloistered nuns within. They tell me the true sacrifice is to live on the outside, though they do not complain. Inside they could be fully themselves. There is work, of course, much of it hard manual farm labour. But there is one purpose, one focus. Outside, they must play the part of good religious sister for others. Inside there is no gaze except God's gaze.

'AMONG THIS GENERATION is a desire to do big things for God', said Sister Mara Grace, reflecting on the hundreds of conversations she's had with young Catholic women as the vocational director at the convent of Nashville Dominicans. 'Gen Z has big questions. They want to live life that is authentic, and tried and true.'

In 2006, the Nashville Dominicans had 200 sisters. Today, they have 318 sisters, ranging in age from 18 to 96. Though active and not cloistered (the sisters work outside the convent after completing years of religious formation), they wear a full traditional habit, live in community and chant the daily Divine Office, bucking post-Vatican II trends towards deregulation. The community receives 500 inquiries a year, half from women under the age of 18. Every year 5 to 15 women take perpetual vows, after a demanding process that requires 8 years of living in the convent.

There are at least 17 different orders of cloistered or contemplative nuns in the United States, spanning 300 monasteries and housing about 4,000 nuns. Every order is distinct: the austere Poor Clares are proudly communal, while Carmelites, by far the largest with 63 monasteries, emphasise solitude and mental prayer. Benedictines are musical. Each order has its own schedule, habit, norms and history. Some wake every day at 3:30am for the morning office, and others at 4:30am, 5am or 6am. Some pray in the middle of the night. Their habits can be white, brown, gray, black, red, or even pink. Some, like the historically welcoming Order of the Visitation, are diminishing and others, such as the unbending Norbertines, are opening in the United States for the first time.

Just outside Fresno, in northern California, the hard-to-find Norbertine monastery has grown from 5 nuns in 2005 to over 50 women in 2024, on 500 acres of remote land. Established in 1120, the cloistered branch of Norbertines values silence, manual labour, and strict seclusion. They are the only monastery to return none of my calls or emails, as family members of nuns inside warned me they might do. They do not advertise and seek no attention. Women arrive through word of mouth. As one mother of a nun put it to me, 'They are the place you go when you want to truly live like the original hermits of God.'

This type of seclusion is not the only way, and many young women are drawn to communities with greater worldly engagement. The Benedictine monastery in Gower, Missouri, which prays the Latin office (many of the monasteries that are growing use the Latin Mass, like other symbols of tradition), has started three new monasteries in the past five years to meet demand. Benedictines are contemplative, not cloistered, meaning nuns can greet outsiders without a separation barrier and even visit family or travel on religious retreat, but their days are regulated by prayer and monastic work.

'We just keep getting more applications every

> *'These women want something heroic. To live here is a sacrifice; it is saying no to the world and all its pleasures.'*
> —*Sister Misericordia*

year,' Sister Misericordia, who entered in 2006, told a Catholic newspaper in May 2024. 'These women want something heroic. To live here is a sacrifice; it is saying no to the world and all its pleasures. To give that up is huge, but these women desire the divine husband and are willing to give everything to be with him.'

It is a trend that might have shocked Catholic officials in the 1960s, when the Second Vatican Council revolutionised the role of Catholic nuns. For the first time since 1298, the nuns were allowed to leave the convent. (Orders of charity work were only considered religious congregations, and members did not take solemn vows.) Monasteries were encouraged to simplify the habits the nuns wore, expand the types of foods they were allowed to eat, and reduce penitential practices, such as wearing hair shirts or flogging themselves. In addition to practical changes, the Council also gave monastic life a new theological foundation. Instead of being uniquely holy and worthy of salvation, the status of the nun became equal to that of a layperson who had simply chosen a worthy vocation, as noble as marriage, but not more. Holiness was now available to everyone. The goal of the Council was to 'open up the windows and let fresh air' into the church. For many, the reforms were long overdue.

Until 1965, nuns needed to ask permission from their superiors for everything from borrowing an extra pen to getting a new bar of soap, often in a humbling process that involved kneeling on the floor (known to this day as 'permissions'). Obedience was paramount. Special friendships of any kind were forbidden – they infringed on one's

> **Cloistered life feels so exciting, even rebellious, to a generation cynical about the future.**

ability to belong uniquely to Jesus – and so silence reigned even during recreational hours, to prevent personal discussions.

Though often painted as medieval, the vast majority of these restrictions had been codified during Vatican I, in 1870, which tried to get ahead of modernising impulses brought on by the Enlightenment. Vatican II returned authority to the monasteries, allowing superiors to adjust daily life to reflect changing norms and the needs of the women inside. As a result, instead of gradual change over the century, a torrent of reforms flooded monasteries all at once. Scores of orders chose to discard their habits, those veils and wimples that marked the nun, and wear respectable, polished clothing instead. After all, the original habits were often nothing more than modest, simple versions of clothing worn by women in the century the order was founded. Many orders disbanded communal living, sending sisters to live on their own in apartments. There

was a wave of optimism for the future, buoyed by the revolutionary spirit of the 1960s. Women's liberation and the fight for civil rights gave many people hope that they could build a better future, if only they would throw off the evils of the past.

In the decade that followed, thousands of nuns left the convents and monasteries – more than 4,000 in 1970 alone.

For some, there was not enough reform, after a century of promise and progress. Women still had no formal power in the church. For others, the loss of traditional life was too great to bear. Nuns were asked to review the rituals, rules and restrictions that governed their lives. Some welcomed the prospect, but others felt unequal to such a weighty task. What gave their lives meaning if not living an unquestioned, ancient way of life?

By the 1970s, active orders such as the Sisters of Mercy had become the public face of consecrated life, if one thought about nuns at all. Like Catholic priests, active sisters live consecrated lives under vows but still buy groceries, drive cars, listen to music and live in the world. The shift to private homes and everyday clothing felt emblematic of a new era, where women could serve God as they were and without the requirement to live under supervision.

By the 1990s, however, the enthusiasm of the 1960s had given way to conservatism and debates around monastic life dropped from public life. Since nuns were no longer recognisable on the street, many assumed they had gone the way of hatpins and telegrams. To this day, people are surprised to learn there are still monasteries in the United States, active or cloistered.

This is perhaps one reason cloistered life feels so exciting, even rebellious, to a generation cynical about the future. It is a rejection of the world, a way to pull one's investments from society and bet everything on God, the ultimate act of defiance. The cloister can seem like a forgotten solution to modern problems, hidden away in the history of the church. This ancient

history also gives it legitimacy and the assurance that its meaning will outlive any modern notions of right and wrong.

'In the past 15 years, there has been a culture of discernment developing,' said Sister Jacinta, who grew up in Princeton, New Jersey, and dropped out of New York University in 2010 to join the Nashville Dominicans. Her postulant class was 27 women, of whom 13 took perpetual vows 8 years later. 'If you're a young, faithful Catholic, the question of vocation and discernment comes up naturally today.'

Indeed, organisations and groups for women discerning monastic life have proliferated. Finding information on monasteries used to be difficult, especially for smaller and lesser-known orders, such as the Passionists or the Pink Sisters. Today, such information is all over the internet, and many monasteries have a website, sometimes even a contact form. Discernment booths are prevalent at Catholic college conferences.

Earlier generations of nuns struggled with a feeling that they were sitting on the sidelines of history, sequestered away in their monasteries as important societal changes brewed. In the wake of women's liberation, many young Catholic women saw cloistered life as redolent of the past, part and parcel of a world that confined women to the home and hid them from society. These are not burdens that most Catholic women carry today. Instead, the

> **The intensity of cloistered life is seen as freedom from a world often bereft of meaning or true, deep faith.**

intensity of cloistered life is seen as freedom from a world often bereft of meaning or true, deep faith. The monastery is freedom. If once austerity was imposed on nuns, today it is freely chosen.

'I feel so much more free now than I ever did in the world, even though we don't go anywhere,' Sister Rosalie Agnes told me. 'Carmel is so big spiritually that you don't need all the rest of the world, because you have so much just right in front of you.'

Monastic trends have always oscillated between expansion and reform. In the 11th and 12th centuries, monastic life grew until it became lax with numbers, prompting the papal restrictions of the 13th and 14th centuries. The mendicant orders brought concern about enclosure and education levels among monks, bringing openness and then backlash. From the Benedictines came the Camaldolese, and then the Cistercians, from whom came the more stringent Trappists. Many orders have a 'Reformed' branch, pointing to a time when a group of monks or nuns decided they needed to return to the original, most austere ways. Today, the Reformed branches outpace the original ones. Always there is someone to go off to the forest and say, 'I want it starker, harder, realer.' And then more people join them, the community grows more permissive as it grows wider, and the process starts anew.

This doesn't mean there are no hurdles. Nothing is more traditional than the monastic vocation in Catholic life, yet conservative religious culture in America is particularly centred on family, and values women who are mothers. Choosing a life without the possibility of marriage and motherhood is hard to champion. American Catholics also tend to have smaller families than the historically larger Catholic families where a daughter could go off to the convent and leave her remaining eight siblings to care for her parents. For many only children, the vocational calling can be a knife to the heart, as they know how painful it will be for their parents.

There is also the American focus on productivity and efficiency. Here, the mysteries of the cloister become all the more compelling – even divine. Brother Paul Quenon, a monk in the Gethsemani monastery in Kentucky, titled his 2018 memoir *In Praise of the Useless Life*. M Basil Pennington, a cloistered monk writing from his Massachusetts monastery in 1992, described monasticism as 'a luxurious life …[in which] men and women with an abundance of gifts and talents which could well be employed for the good of the church and the poor sit in the idleness of contemplation.' Thomas Merton, the prolific Trappist monk who died in 1968, evoked the concept when defending the extreme ways of sixth-century Byzantine ascetics, who lived on tall pillars. 'We treat their lives as absurd and grotesque,' Merton wrote in his journals. 'But this is not the full truth. It was a witness to the divine transcendency. Precisely its uselessness is what made this witness powerful.'

The nuns who continue to answer such a call are a powerful witness, and it is a call that will never cease crying out.

Good Cops

As my town's police chief, I want my work to focus on relationships, not statistics.

JOHN CLAIR

A COUPLE OF YEARS AGO, when I was serving as chief of police of Quantico, Virginia, I found myself picking up trash in Raftelis Park, alongside a guy in his 20s who, his tattoos told me, was involved in gang activity. We weren't far from FBI headquarters: in Quantico, you never are. But there he was, that day of the annual town clean-up event, no enmity between us. I'm not an FBI guy, I'm regular old police. We picked trash in silence for a while, the Potomac River that borders the park flowing beside us, then fell into companionable conversation. From what I knew – and I did know something of his activities – my park clean-up buddy wasn't involved in

John Clair is the chief of police in Marion, Virginia, USA, where he lives with his wife and four children. He has over 20 years of law enforcement experience, and serves on the executive board of the Virginia Association of Chiefs of Police.

criminal activity in my town, but only when he was in a nearby jurisdiction. And he didn't want to live in a town whose parks were filled with garbage any more than I did. He didn't want to live in an unsafe neighbourhood, either, or one where people and the police are at odds.

The job of the police is something like repair. Of course we have to solve crime, catch bad guys. But when the social fabric gets frayed it is both a cause of and a result of crime. Our job is to do our best to repair that fabric, weaving together the threads of reparative justice for victims, and restorative justice for perpetrators, bringing them back into the community.

We forget this pretty frequently, and the way that police are trained tends to promote that forgetting. We are too often trained as technocrats: human relationships are not legible to the programmes and statistical models and paperwork that are the tools of contemporary policing.

But they're what the job should be all about.

Law enforcement in the United States is still searching for a firm footing in the post-2020 landscape, rocked by protests after the murder of George Floyd. The so-called Ferguson Effect (named for a similar dynamic following the 2014 shooting of Michael Brown in Ferguson, Missouri) has led to a pull-back on police presence in communities and subsequent rise in crime. Floundering, we question what we thought were the principles of our job.

In trying to find a way forward, some have looked to the past, with the refrain, 'We just need to get cops back on the beat.' Others point to Robert Peel's 1829 principles of policing, as if Victorian-era policing ideals describe and prescribe all the tasks of contemporary police. Some hang their hats on shibboleths like 'procedural justice' – which, important as it is, can become its own form of technocracy, something we use to protect ourselves: if we do the procedures right, no one can blame us, even if justice itself is elusive.

Still, these ideas – beat-cop, shoe-leather community policing and care with procedures – are at least good in themselves, even if they're not enough. More concerning is the turn to high-tech approaches to police-community relations – 'there's an app for that' – a reliance on technology and data that fails to capture the human contours of actual experience or rebuild trust.

WHAT DOES THIS look like? I recently Zoomed into a town-hall forum, full of residents and desperate elected officials, as part of a police executive search process. Violence in the community had been spiking, and these residents wanted to know what the new executive would do to address it. It was a profoundly human moment. 'Can you make us safe?' the residents were saying. 'Can we trust that you will neither neglect nor abuse us?'

The job candidate met those questions by mentioning CompStat. Short for computer statistics, this is a technique of data-gathering and assessment used to develop crime response strategies; it was first used in New York City in the 1990s. To my mind, the candidate had answered 'Can you make us safe?' with 'We'll have to crunch the numbers.' This did not alleviate the tension of the conversation.

The truth is that police departments are increasingly becoming organisationally schizophrenic. In the corridors of police agencies across the nation, leaders are internally moving away from the calculated management practices of the past, but in our relations with the community, we're working on a technocratic model. We've started to humanise ourselves, while continuing to mechanise our interactions with the people we're meant to serve.

Essentially, this is the law-enforcement version of Taylorism. The 'scientific management' approach of F W Taylor, now more than a century old, is grounded in the belief that *efficiency* is the highest goal of workplace culture. Each person in an organisation must work in such a way as to be as interchangeable and frictionless as possible. In the factories in which Taylorism was first applied, this meant that workers were almost literally reduced to cogs in the machine. In the white-collar workplaces to which it was later extended, 'leadership' was replaced with 'management', and management was meant to be as impersonal as possible: data-driven and mechanical.

Taylor famously used a method that deconstructed work, identified primary tasks, and timed those tasks, then instructed workers in the precise way in which they must move their bodies to perform the tasks for maximum production speed. Production went up, but humanity went down.

If you do this enough, you stop being a man who is using a technique and become a thing used by it.

Delve into any of the disheartening literature related to police technology initiatives and this bleak vision will be apparent: the overwhelming goal is efficiency.

What does this look like? You get officers driving city streets, the screens in their cars running green with waterfalls of numbers. They are looking for glitches in the social matrix. They see themselves as people among numbers, people among tasks, people among objects and people among clusters of catalogued and bundled behaviour.

This is what policing looks like when we see our communities through the lens of data – it's all about moving the numbers. This is how humans are legible to the technology we use, including the social technology of scientific management.

Pick up some of the textbooks on crime, read some of the journals, read the promotional material for the latest seminar or system, and you will be hard-pressed to find any discussion of crimes – the stories of people and justice and pain.

Spring 2025 81

What you will find instead is all about crime rates. We talk in terms of crimes per capita – number of murders per 100,000 in population. That is, by itself, as useless a way to think about the citizens and victims and criminals and suspects who are your community as it would be to consider that the national average birth rate is 1.94 children per couple as you are making decisions for your own family. Instinctively everyone knows this, but once this type of thinking becomes entrenched, a more humane alternative seems unimaginable.

Years ago, when I was a patrol-man, my supervisor warned me that my 'ticket numbers were low.' He was not claiming that traffic accidents, fatalities, or complaints had risen. There was no tangible problem in my patrol area that he could point to. Rather, I'd failed to meet a specified target, decided in the abstract, for effective patrol techniques. This wasn't a conversation about the condition of the community; it was a conversation about measurement. My supervisor was a technocrat, and I was being optimised.

Meanwhile in my patrol area, I had far more important issues to deal with than attempting to collect a random spattering of traffic tickets to satisfy some metric on a spreadsheet. I had lots of people problems. I was dealing with victims of domestic violence, violent crime, gang activity and robbery. I could name them. I didn't have a problem with traffic victims that the emphasis on tickets might (most charitably) be intended to solve, but I did have real people who needed real help. I tried to explain these things. I could see his eyes glaze over during my sermon – in his mind I was simply lazy. If only I would bring the numbers up, I'd be lauded as an effective contributor to the team effort, irrespective of the actual outcomes.

This is the type of environment that makes cops hate our jobs. And the dehumanisation it fosters too easily gets passed on, leading us to despise the integers (the citizens) who compose the equation (the community). It's a context that cannot help but generate enmity. Police learn to see ourselves as fulfillers of quotas, targets and goals. The public are the units we use to quantify those targets. There is no dignity, no honour, in either role.

Many police executives are aware of this tendency. We try. Often we will add a footnote to data-driven discussions: 'Remember, each one of these numbers is a real person.' Or, as I heard in a recent public information training I attended, 'Communication is a value, not a technique.' This was followed by several hours of training in communication techniques. Ultimately, these caveats ring hollow. After all, if we really believed in the humans behind the numbers, their humanity would go without saying.

This must change. Good teaching is not teaching to the test; good policing is not policing to the metrics.

The technocratic ideal becomes most obvious, and can be most destructive, in police-hiring ideology. This type of thinking usually expresses itself via some type of euphemism like 'he can do the job', or 'he can handle himself', both of which are another way of saying, 'despite what might be serious character flaws, this applicant can fulfill the transactional task.' Skills first, humanity second. The idea that a good policeman must first be a good man is often alien to our hiring practices. We've all seen the tragic outcomes associated with this type of hiring, in the shocking encounters between police officers and suspects (or even random bystanders) that regularly make the news.

To solve the problem of police alienation from the community, we simply have to stop framing our world according to it. We have to realise we are literally speaking the problem of police–community separation into existence, creating our own inhumane reality, one data-driven meeting at a time. We have to become radically person-centred and, in particular, victim-centred. Meetings related to crime control in a community must involve the community openly, transparently, and frequently.

We should all be sitting at the same table, seeking solutions together. We need to be talking with those who live with our decisions.

THESE DAYS I'M THE CHIEF of police in Marion, Virginia, in the heart of Appalachia. A long way from Quantico, a long way from anywhere. Mountains rise up behind the main street.

When I arrived in Marion six years ago, I started scouting the community for applicants for the department. I found a young man working at a local hardware store. It wasn't a great job, didn't pay much, but he had one of the most compelling customer service attitudes I've ever seen. He had a second gig, part-time at a local Mexican restaurant, where he was its only non-Hispanic employee. I immediately recognised the strengths associated with someone who could not only thrive in a public-facing customer service job, but also seamlessly integrate into a diverse work setting. I hired that young man about a year later.

A couple of years ago, this officer encountered a man with a hunting bow. He was aiming for something like suicide by cop, determined to either kill or be killed. Bulletproof vests are not knife-proof or arrow-proof. The officer was in mortal danger and would have been, by standard measures, justified in killing the man. He did not. He recognised the humanity of his assailant, and took every possible action to avoid bloodshed at the risk of his own life. With this approach, he may well have saved two lives.

This story about defusing a violent encounter is what policing should look like in almost every case. It won't always end this way. But we can at least strive to make encounters that end in deadly force true anomalies.

Within the safety that effective and humane protection against crime can offer, the social

Spring 2025   83

fabric can be repaired. In Marion we have a grassroots initiative launched by local leaders called The Appalachian Center for Hope. The ACH's stated goal is to provide a whole-community and cross-sector response to the crisis of addiction – primarily opioid addiction – in our region. We've recognised that as a community, we can't arrest or regulate our way out of the problems associated with addiction. We can, however, rally around those affected and support them – providing secure bridges from one step of recovery to the next.

> **Ultimately, police are secondary: they repair, but it is others who weave. The social fabric must, if it is to be repaired, first exist.**

Ultimately, police are secondary: they repair, but it is others who weave. The social fabric must, if it is to be repaired, first exist. That's the work first of parents, who raise human beings; of teachers and students, employers and employees, lodge brothers and volunteers, hobbyists and dog owners. When the just life they are living with each other, the justice they are giving to each other in each interaction, is interrupted by a crime, a violation of justice, police can and must step in, but only to restore what was already there.

To counter the forces of dehumanisation – not just in policing, but modern life in general – I recommend the 'integral humanism' described by mid-century Catholic philosopher Jacques Maritain and popularised by figures such as C S Lewis and T S Eliot. This vision of order recognises a complex, combined human reality, honouring our shared place in the created cosmos, integrating the very best of what we have produced in helping us navigate it – together.

'If', Maritain wrote in *Humanisme Intégral* (1936), 'instead of resting in the heart, purity rises to the head, it creates sectarians and heretics.' Our job as police is to promote safety and justice in a community, among humans who are spiritual as well as physical and intellectual beings. We have to treat them, and ourselves, as the kinds of creatures we are. The problems we face in law-enforcement interactions are not going to be solved by the adoption of mechanical catechisms of 'procedure', or the recasting of the ideals of order, or by CompStat – these may help tactically, but not strategically. If we are going to police well, we must police human beings, not statistical agglomerations. We must know that we ourselves are flawed human beings, of the same kind as those we are entrusted to guard.

That day in the park in Quantico with the gang member was formative for me. The man I was working beside wanted to live in a good place, just as I did. We were working towards that goal together.

Several weeks later he was arrested in town, on a warrant for crimes committed elsewhere. As soon as he was released, he returned to Quantico and came to the police station. He asked to speak to me. He apologised: he had shamed himself in my eyes. This floored me. Somehow, he viewed our relationship in different terms than he did his relationship with other police officers. I can only think the reason was that to him, I wasn't just a cop. He saw me as a fellow human, just as I did him.

A cynic might not make much of this story, but I took from it hope. Perhaps for the first time in his life, he had experienced the fellowship of common work with a police officer, and in that context, wanted to become a vital part of an ordered community. We were both invested, shoulder to shoulder. Maybe, as a start, it can be that simple.

COMMUNITY SNAPSHOT

The Rewards of Elder Care

At the Bruderhof, I've learned that caregiving is not a one-way street.

MAUREEN SWINGER

THE FIRST ELDERLY PERSON I cared for was my own grandmother, Anni. I had adored her from my earliest memories – in fact, my actual earliest memory. When I was three, my baby brother was very sick. While my parents spent weeks in and out of the hospital with him, I camped with Oma Anni. She had a quaint little trundle bed that rolled out from under her bouncy grandmother bed, and I slept near her, after three other very important events had occurred – a nightly reading from Johanna Spyri's *Heidi*, a *bettmümpfeli* (apparently Swiss for bedtime snack), and then, rather than lullabies, songs of praise, sometimes accompanied by her

---

Maureen Swinger is an editor at Plough and lives at the Fox Hill Bruderhof in Walden, New York, with her husband, Jason, and their three children.

An elderly woman joins a beach outing with the help of family and carers at the Beech Grove Bruderhof in Kent, United Kingdom.

quiet guitar. They were in German or Schweizer-deutsch, but I recognised a common thread: *Jesu – Schönster Herr Jesu*. I fell asleep under a blanket of benediction.

As she entered her 90s, I offered to care for her in turn. I was in my early 20s and we had not lived together in years, but she still thought I was her little Swiss Miss. You wouldn't know she was growing more forgetful except on occasion, such as the first time she turned on her lamp in the middle of the night to go to the toilet. Because she

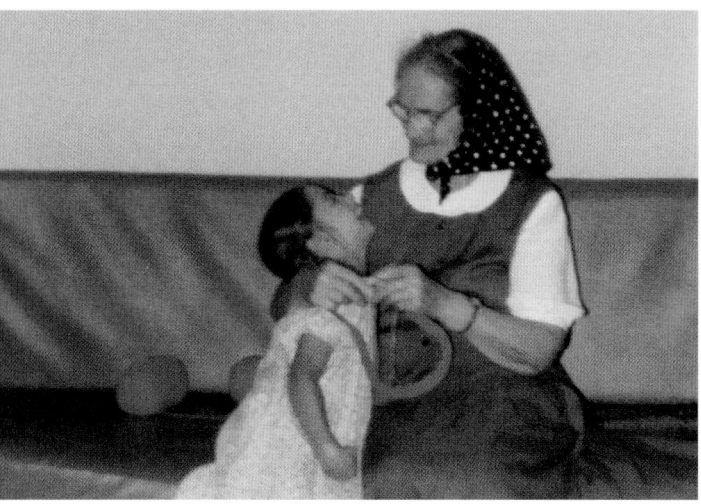

had become so unsteady on her feet and didn't care for the idea of a walker, I was sleeping in the same room to be at her elbow as soon as she stood up. When she beheld me hastily mobilising, she gave a surprised but delighted smile – 'Ach, that's right! You are camping with me. Just like olden times!' We went arm in arm down the hall and back, and she kissed me good night.

The next night, I awoke to stealthy movements in the dark. She was putting on her dressing gown and tiptoeing towards the door. I jumped up with alacrity, and she expressed some mild dismay – 'I was trying not to disturb your sleep!' We had the gentlest of arguments as to my true purpose for camping, and from then on, she accepted the nightly company with good grace. I realised later that she accepted everything with an uncommon amount of grace.

She took every day as something of a celebration. I never once heard a word of anger or criticism towards anyone. We had many cups of tea, much laughter over small daily happenings and sometimes just times of quietly being together. She died as gracefully as she had lived, stepping eagerly across a threshold to be with *Schönster Herr Jesu*.

How I hope I will inherit her grace when I am old. I know that my mother will and that I most likely won't. My carers will probably have to

---

Until our society attributes far greater value both to carers and those who need care, families will continue to operate in an hour-to-hour survival mode.

---

acquire patience they didn't know they had, just as I had to with the next elderly lady I looked after, who was irked at needing to depend on anyone. I'll call her June. I was never fast enough for her, or very good at perceiving needs: the room was not warm enough, or it was too warm. How come her favourite blanket was in the wash again? Why did we have to go out for fresh air? Didn't I know that one could die from exposure to too much fresh air? Always exhausted, she planned three naps into each day, so the corresponding nights only continued the cycle of catnaps and complaints. It was eye-opening to find out that not every old lady was Oma Anni, and soul-opening to realise that this Oma needed love just as much, or even more.

Now that I'm no longer in my 20s, and have had to face some chronic health issues myself, I wish I had seen June

The author with her grandmother Anni, as a child (above) and as an adult carer (opposite).

more clearly: her dignity, her personhood, her fears. My grandmother did not fear death; she was peaceably counting the days till she could cross over. June did not seem to fear death either, but with every breath, she was battling the process of dying with its spiral of loss – loss of agency, ability, visibility. This must have been terrifying.

It can be a different kind of terrifying to be a carer, especially if you have no respite from a difficult, frequently thankless task. It's hard enough when you're earning a living caring for a stranger. Your day's work can include anxious or irritable patients, backbreaking lifting, contact with body fluids. And for all this effort you might get minimum wage.

But when it's a relative, and you are her round-the-clock attendant with no backup in sight, it's hard in other ways, with love and gratitude and grief and role-reversals tangled in the mix. No matter who it is, though, here we stand, like Sisyphus staring up the mountain every damned morning. Any distance we may have pushed the rock yesterday must be slogged through all over again today, and the rock seems to be getting heavier every time.

I don't believe elder care is truly tenable for one nuclear family, let alone one person. If we honour God's image in each human being, especially in the frail, we ought to honour it together. Yet until our society attributes far greater value both to carers and those who need care, families will continue to operate in an hour-to-hour survival pattern. Nursing homes will continue to be understaffed and underfunded. Carers will continue to burn out. If society is failing to meet these needs, what other options are there?

A strong case could be made for compensation, perhaps funds made available for those who work to care for a relative, both to acknowledge that it *is* work and to make it possible for more people to do it. But while this could help support families trying to manage on their own, no amount of money can truly capture the value of this care.

And increasingly as the years go by, more elderly people are family-less, never having had children who might care for them in their old age. They have no network to uphold them, financially or otherwise.

Care fatigue can happen even when there is a support structure in place. Within the Bruderhof, the intentional Christian community I belong to, there's a fairly robust structure. Members live together on intergenerational campuses, and most of us are tasked with caring for an elderly person at

some point in our lives. Acts 4 is a central tenet of our church: 'And God's grace was so powerfully at work in them all that there were no needy persons among them.' We might not always feel God's grace as powerfully as did the early apostles, but we can believe in it, and work so that no one is lonely or neglected. It's still hard, but it's doable; we have others to lean on. We promise to care for each other as brothers and sisters, and we trust we will be cared for in turn.

Each Bruderhof community assigns a team to look out for the needs of its inhabitants, every family and member. When someone needs more active care, whether a daytime or live-in arrangement, there will be a discussion as to who can best step up. Such a request doesn't come as a total surprise to the person called upon – when we join, we promise to serve wherever the community needs us most. We might not like the timing, but we can't beg off just because we already have a day job. If people are to be prioritised over profit, the income-earning workforce will take a hit – several hits. Even worthy ventures such as *Plough* might have to take second place. (At the Bruderhof, we don't take home individual salaries – any income is shared among the whole community – so the trade-offs that many other families experience between earning a living and supporting a frail relative are alleviated.)

This care doesn't require much medical expertise; our onsite medical team checks in with anyone who is ageing and calls on specialists for more critical health needs. The carers assist in the tasks of daily living, in the minutiae that are sometimes awkward, often messy. Often beautiful as well.

There are other churches and congregations that work to set up care networks, or support and relieve families who are navigating full-time care situations. But they also face the quandary of a limited workforce and shifting commitments. I don't know how this model might be extrapolated into wider society, but if change is to come, it will have to be through example, and some of the best examples are to be found in circles of faith.

JASON AND I HAD BEEN MARRIED a few weeks when we were asked to look after Doug and Ruby. We had demanding jobs, worked with the community youth group, and had just discovered our first child was on the way, but we were game to try. Besides, 20 years before, Ruby had been my English teacher and I would be forever thankful for her interest and inspiration.

Newlyweds and octogenarians – that was a new dance for both parties. There were a few missteps as we all found our groove, but really, there were

---

In our first year of marriage we did not get romantic evenings and scenic outings. We got a training in what makes a real marriage.

---

no great challenges for Jason and me; it was simply a matter of putting their needs first.

One could argue that the first year of marriage should be about getting to know each other, spending romantic evenings and taking scenic outings. We did not get that. We got a training in what makes a real marriage. Whatever was happening, Doug and Ruby each thought first about how it would affect the other. Ruby often had trouble sleeping and Doug read her Elizabeth Goudge novels by the hour. Sometimes they sat together in companionable silence, needing not a word between them. Sixty-three years of marriage, three stillborn children, three living children, two of them adopted. Grief and joy, the span of a whole life lived in search of faith and truth – what words still needed to be said?

The four of us started and ended our days with a reading and a prayer. Sometimes Doug had a tip or two for us, sometimes Ruby and I talked books

Doug and Ruby in 2004.

till a little bit past bedtime (or a lot). We didn't know that they were in their final months. Ruby died soon after a stroke and her family included us in all the final gestures of love, as we set up the wake, brought in sheaves of the lilacs blooming outside her window and pinned tributes from former students on the walls.

Doug outlived her by a few months, grieving, hurting, sometimes abrupt or peremptory in his pain. Even though he had family nearby, he was unhappy if we were out in the evenings, so we stayed close. He often spoke about Ruby, of the many ways he knew he would miss her and all the little things that still surprised him every day about her absence. We felt impossibly young and inadequate, yet honoured to listen.

EIGHTEEN YEARS LATER, Doug and Ruby remain in my heart, along with the others we've cared for since then. Some were easier than others. I have found the physical side of caring much less difficult than looking after someone with dementia. It hurts viscerally to see a vibrant being going grey, no longer recognising her loved ones, lashing out, not against people but against the encroaching emptiness.

I think of these experiences now when I encounter Friede. She has always had a regal bearing; as a child I thought her beautiful and a bit fierce. She loved in an expansive way, yet sometimes seemed aloof. Now she has advanced dementia and needs a sturdy team of young women (some trained nurses, some natural carers) to help with bathing, eating and getting out of bed. It is not at all easy, and they have set up a rotation so they can look after her well, and take breaks between.

I'm not part of that care team, but I see Friede every day. Whenever she catches someone's eye, she says, 'I love you', and she wants to hear it in return. If you are within reach, you will be pulled close with surprising strength, for a hug or a resounding kiss. These are not hard to give or receive. Her eyes still flash brilliantly and I think she must still remember her people, the ones she used to boss around lovingly years ago. But there's no way to tell. Her own brothers and sisters have all died, so the people within range are all she has.

One evening in December, when my youngest daughter got back from singing carols at a local nursing home, she was pensive. When I asked her what was up, she told me, 'There were no decorations in their rooms. There was no way to

know it was Christmas. I think our songs were the only thing.' She felt lonely on their behalf, and wondered where their families were.

The next day I met Friede, accompanied by two of her faithful attendants, and we exchanged another hug. I couldn't help wondering if this was her last Christmas. Either way, she was living it up, travelling everywhere under a festive red blanket, eyes sparkling at the lights, singing carols with words and tunes that have not yet deserted her. She knows what love is, and her carers do too. It's in every lift, every spoonful of breakfast, every bleary day that follows a busy night, every burst of unexpected laughter, every wordless tear. It is her family.

Friede reading to some young friends.

READINGS

Vincent van Gogh, *Enclosed Field with Ploughman*, oil on canvas, 1889

Created for Work

Dorothy L Sayers
Miroslav Volf
Leo Tolstoy
Francis of Assisi

Dorothy L Sayers (1893–1957) was a British writer best known for her detective stories as well as for her translation of Dante's Divine Comedy.

IN NOTHING has the church so lost her hold on reality as in her failure to understand and respect the secular vocation. She has allowed work and religion to become separate departments, and is astonished to find that, as a result, the secular work of the world is turned to purely selfish and destructive ends, and that the greater part of the world's intelligent workers have become irreligious, or at least, uninterested in religion.

But is it astonishing? How can any one remain interested in a religion which seems to have no concern with nine-tenths of his life? The church's approach to an intelligent carpenter is usually confined to exhorting him not to be drunk and disorderly in his leisure hours, and to come to church on Sundays. What the church should be telling him is this: that the very first demand that his religion makes upon him is that he should make good tables.

Dorothy L Sayers, *Letters to a Diminished Church* (W Publishing Group, 2004) 131–132.

Miroslav Volf (b. 1956) is a theologian and public intellectual, and the founding director of the Yale Center for Faith and Culture.

IF THE PURPOSE of human life is either reflection (as in much of philosophical tradition) or worship (as in much of Christian tradition), then work can have only instrumental value. One works in order to keep alive, and one lives in order to think or worship. But if work is a fundamental dimension of human existence, then work cannot have only an instrumental value. If God's purpose for human beings is not only for them to ensure that certain states of affairs come about (the cultivation and preservation of the Garden of Eden) but that these states of affairs are created through human work (tilling and keeping), then work cannot be only a means to life whose purpose exists fully in something outside work, but must be considered an aspect of the purpose of life itself. If I am created to work, then I must treat work as something I am created to do and hence (at least partly) treat it as an end in itself.

Therefore, a person cannot live a fully human existence if she refuses to work. This is not the same as saying that she is not fully human if she does not work! For then the aged and ill who can no longer work, and small children who cannot yet work, would not be fully human. Because humanity is exclusively a gift from God, a person can be fully human without working, but because God gave him humanity partly in order to work, he cannot live as fully human without working. It is, therefore, contrary to the purpose of human life to reduce work to a mere means of subsistence. One should not turn a fundamental aspect of life into a mere means of life. Just as the whole of human life is an end in itself – without, of course, ceasing to be a means to glorify God and benefit the creation – so also must work, as a fundamental dimension of human life, be an end in itself.

Miroslav Volf, *Work in the Spirit: Toward a Theology of Work* (Wipf and Stock, 2001) 197. Used by permission of Wipf and Stock Publishers, *wipfandstock.com*.

Leo Tolstoy (1828–1910) was a Russian writer best known for his novels, War and Peace *and* Anna Karenina.

Another inevitable condition of happiness is work: first, the intellectual labour that one is free to choose and loves; secondly, the exercise of physical power that brings a good appetite and tranquil and profound sleep. Here, again, the greater the imagined prosperity that falls to the lot of men according to the doctrine of the world, the more such men are deprived of this condition of happiness. All the prosperous people of the world, the men of dignity and wealth, are as completely deprived of the advantages of work as if they were shut up in solitary confinement. They struggle unsuccessfully with the diseases caused by the need of physical exercise, and with the ennui which pursues them – unsuccessfully, because labour is a pleasure only when it is necessary, and they have need of nothing; or they undertake work that is odious to them, like the bankers, solicitors, administrators, and government officials, and their wives, who plan receptions and routs and devise toilettes for themselves and their children. (I say odious, because I never yet met any person of this class who was contented with his work or took as much satisfaction in it as the porter feels in shovelling away the snow from before their doorsteps.) All these favourites of fortune are either deprived of work or are obliged to work at what they do not like, after the manner of criminals condemned to hard labour.

Leo Tolstoy, *What I Believe,* trans. Huntington Smith (Thomas Y. Crowell, 1885), 187.

Vincent van Gogh, *Sower at Sunset*, oil on canvas, 1888.

Francis of Assisi (c. 1181–1226) was an Italian mystic and Catholic friar who founded the religious order of the Franciscans.

LET THE BROTHERS in whatever places they may be among others to serve or to work, not be chamberlains, nor cellarers, nor overseers in the houses of those whom they serve, and let them not accept any employment which might cause scandal, or be injurious to their soul, but let them be inferior and subject to all who are in the same house.

And let the brothers who know how to work labour and exercise themselves in that art they may understand, if it be not contrary to the salvation of their soul, and they can exercise it becomingly. For the prophet says: 'For thou shalt eat the labours of thy hands; blessed art thou, and it shall be well with thee'; and the apostle: 'If any man will not work, neither let him eat.' And let every man abide in the art or employment wherein he was called. And for their labour they may receive all necessary things, except money. And if they be in want, let them seek for alms like other brothers. And they may have the tools and implements necessary for their work. Let all the brothers apply themselves with diligence to good works, for it is written: 'Be always busy in some good work, that the devil may find thee occupied'; and again: 'Idleness is an enemy to the soul.' Therefore the servants of God ought always to continue in prayer or in some other good work.

The Writings of Saint Francis of Assisi, newly translated into English with an Introduction and Notes by Father Paschal Robinson (The Dolphin Press, 1906).

Vincent van Gogh, *Corn Harvest in Provence*, oil on canvas, 1888.

Sailing with the Greeks

ADAM NICOLSON

At sea in a small boat, I taste Homer's kind of freedom.

I REMEMBER ONE MORNING, a few years ago, when I felt as happy and free as I ever have. It was early May, I was alone in the Hebrides, and had launched my small wooden boat into the quiet waters of a loch on the east coast of Harris. The boat itself was a perfect thing, 16 feet long, wide in the beam, with a hull made of larch boards on an oak frame. It had a single dipping lugsail whose ochre fabric, when the wind filled it, stretched from the bow almost to the stern in one long sickle-curve above me. I could sit there, one hand on the tiller, the other on the mainsheet, and watch this beautiful form driving the boat onward as if by hidden magic.

Adam Nicolson has written numerous books on landscape, literature, history, and the sea. His most recent book is How to Be: Life Lessons from the Early Greeks *(Farrar, Straus and Giroux, 2023). He and his wife live in Sussex, England.*

Collage with photograph of the author sailing a small Hebridean lugger called *Broad Bay* in the Minch, a strait on the west coast of Scotland, with the Shiant Islands in the background. All photographs by James Nutt.

Out of the loch, a light breeze came in over my left shoulder. I had about 15 miles of sea to cross but the boat cut its way easily through the mildly rippled surface of the Minch. The sea was sparkling in the sunshine and I had to squeeze my eyes against the little shafts of sun coming off each wave. A pair of pale, scarred Risso's dolphins swept past me, curving up and down together, breathing as they rose. A long black minke whale slid through, as dark as the sea itself, easing away to the south. Above it, kittiwakes and a great skua flickered and turned across the perfect seascape.

Long swells were creaming in from the north, each a hundred yards from crest to crest and about eight feet high. At one point they rose over a hidden rock ridge into a band of surf half a mile long. In the sunshine it looked Hawaiian, a gleaming white brow of breaking sea. I kept to the south of it and pushed on and across the sea as if it were a kind of downland on the move. The tide was carrying us with it, running at the flood, as much as three knots in places, bubbling occasionally into flat mushrooms of upwelling water where the submarine topography had disturbed the flow.

It was a morning of ecstatic ease. The sea and wind were sliding me to my destination and the long-limbed stirring of the boat for these three or four incomparable hours on the wide Atlantic became for me the model of life in an accommodating world.

The beauties of sailing, particularly in a small boat, are dependent on that kind of mobility and fluidity. Nothing is fixed. The boat moves, the helmsman moves within the boat, the sea and wind move, the sail, sheets and rudder all move. Their arrangement is only coherent at each particular moment. A set-up that works for a minute or two will not continue to work as the wind shifts and the sea changes. Fluidity is all, and it may be that the sense of wholeness that comes with sailing when it is as perfect as this is a product of that sequence of temporary and transient solutions. It feels like flight, or like the dream of Icarus.

A paradox is in play. Nothing could be less free than sailing out to sea in a small boat. You are subject to all kinds of disciplines. The sea itself is unreliable. You are never quite sure that your rig and hull are all they should be, nor that you are up to coping with the uncertainties the process will throw at you. It is as dangerous as rock climbing. And yet, out of that cage of uncertainty, if you manage at the helm to find the right solutions and have learned to know the realities by which you are surrounded, a sensation emerges of unparalleled freedom.

I am not entirely sure why this should be. An unstable boat with a flighty rig is not where the culture has most often looked for certainty or comfort. The contemporary German philosopher Peter Sloterdijk has pointed to the fact that most Western philosophy has turned to the solidity of the earth as a place in which to understand and feel good about life. Philosophers, he says, have elaborated a 'general world soil' as part of an overall 'terranism' on which to base their thinking. Western thought has been on a long campaign to establish 'foundations' for what it does. No thought can be valid without some meaty 'groundwork' having been laid. 'Grounds' are where truth is thought to begin.

But maybe the philosophers have been wrong about this? What if, Sloterdijk asks, we substituted 'marinism' for 'terranism?' If we all became marinists, the search for 'bedrock concepts' would be over. No one would be interested in ultimate destinies. Movement and the voyage would become the thing. To leave would be as good as to arrive. We would stay mobile.

Sailing on the sea in a small boat is a form not of escape but of submission to those primeval qualities, to the liquidity of things.

'Imagine a philosophy department attuned to the sea,' Brian O'Keeffe, a Barnard College philosopher, has suggested, ruminating on Sloterdijk's idea. It would have constituted itself 'as a swimming faculty, or at least as the port authority of Old Europe.' The philosophy department as the department for maritime affairs; philosophers as harbour masters and ship chandlers; Kant and Hegel in bathing trunks. If one envisaged a 'nautical reformulation of philosophy', Nietzsche's *Gay Science* would presumably be the key text on the philosophical syllabus. 'Send your ships into uncharted seas!' he exclaims. '*Get on the ships! ... The moral earth, too, is round! The moral earth, too, has its antipodes! ... On to the ships, you philosophers!*'

It would be a return to origins. Western philosophy began in the liquid. The sixth and seventh century BC thinkers in Miletus, the great trading and harbour city of Ionia on the eastern shores of the Aegean, all thought the ultimate reality

lay in fluidity. For Thales the underlying frame of existence was in water. For Anaximander, the ur-substance, the stuff from which everything comes, was the *apeiron*. The word means the 'without-limit': what exists before anything that we know and perceive in the world comes into being, the limitless and everlasting reservoir of being, the imagined state of liquid calm, from which everything that is emerges and to which all eventually returns. For Anaximenes, the third of these Milesian thinkers, the first material was neither Thales' water nor Anaximander's *apeiron* but the air itself, which through variations in its density gave rise to all other materials. 'For all things come-to-be from it and into it they are again dissolved.'

Sailing on the sea in a small boat is a form not of escape but of submission to those primeval qualities, to the liquidity of things. It is the water equivalent of going for a walk, with nothing between you and the world as it is. Smallness is important because with the shrinking of the boat comes an expansion of the world. Crossing a stretch of sea that is only 10 or 15 miles wide, or finding one's way down between the islands of a broken archipelago, carefully catching the tide gates as they open, or waiting at anchor for the tide to turn, becomes as much of an adventure as sailing from one ocean shore to another in a boat fitted to the scale of a wider sea. A small boat, in other words, is more like the clothes you wear than a vehicle you inhabit. You have shrugged off 'the earth, earthy' – Saint Paul's description of the first Adam – as something that stultifies and rigidifies and instead find yourself afloat in a kind of liberty.

This form of engagement with the actual is

different from what people have often described as 'the maritime sublime', that sense of excitement at the scale of the sea, its open-endedness, the restraintlessness of being out and away from land. I have never been convinced by it. Conditions at sea are surely less free than those prevailing in a meadow or wood. The land is not cruel in the way the sea can always be. The sea, in many ways, is a tyranny. There is no freedom in the ocean itself. Its only freedom is in the boat and your relationship to it.

Any kind of seamanship that I have learned – and I wouldn't claim much – does at least teach that almost everything that matters happens before you leave. Every sheet and halyard, every reefing line, every shackle, gudgeon and pintle, every bit of clothing to keep you warm and dry must be in as good a state as you can make it. Every flake of acquired understanding has to be in play – what the wind and tide will do, where you can run to if things turn rough, where you can stow food and drink so that it is at hand without leaving the helm. Only then can you set off. Homer knew all about the beauty and holiness of preparation for what he calls 'the salt desert of the sea.' For the great Greek epics, the readying of a ship was a form of liturgy. Every voyage described in Homer begins with that making good of the little wooden world on which the heroes would rely.

This is the paradox: the freedom experienced by the sailor is dependent on observing the disciplines the boat requires. It is a question of trust, knowing that the boat's hull and spars are good while knowing not to overload them in a wind. Knowing not to overreach but to treat the boat kindly and look for safety in the hope that the boat will treat you kindly in return. Being attentive to sea and wind, looking to be slow and careful in every move you make, every trimming of the sails, every tweak on the rudder.

It is the freedom of submission – but what sort of freedom is that? It steps beyond Isaiah Berlin's famous distinction between negative freedom, which is the freedom to do what you feel like doing, whatever the consequences, and positive freedom, the sense of freedom that comes from fulfilling the best of your self, or even your true self. It is more like the idea expressed by the Canadian philosopher Charles Taylor, which he has called 'situated freedom' and which sees 'free activity as grounded in the acceptance of our defining situation. The struggle to be free … is powered by an affirmation of this defining situation as ours.'

This is a dense formulation, filled with paradox, but one that nevertheless understands that freedom is a form of acceptance of the limitations of the circumstances into which we have been thrown. It is not an assertion of the self against those circumstances (whether positively or negatively expressed) but an identification of the self with them. The only freedom can come from recognising the limits of where and what you are. The small sailing boat in a wide sea makes that acceptance particularly easy. When lying on a sofa or having lunch in a restaurant, nothing seems more obvious than our ability to choose. The menu of life encourages the illusion of potency and feeds the arrogance that comes in its wake. The boat is the opposite of that. It imposes a necessary modesty, a submission to the all too obvious reality of the defining situation around you. You can only do what the boat requires you to do. And in that compulsion, mysteriously, a sense of freedom flowers, one in which your life is

Spring 2025   99

momentarily liberated from the need to choose, perhaps even from the need to be or proclaim a self.

No sailing vessels in the Western tradition have been more potent instruments of freedom than the ships belonging to the Phaeacians in the *Odyssey*. When Odysseus is finally cast up on their shore, wrecked by a vicious Poseidon and scarcely alive, he finds himself in the land of master sailors. They look down on him as an amateur and a vagabond, part pirate, part merchant, part failure. Their own fleet is a dream of perfection. So total is their command, so entirely do they give themselves to the practice of sailing, that the ships seem to sail themselves. The hulls seem to know the headings of distant harbours and the ships fly them there at speeds unknown to other nations.

Even in Iron Age Greece, attention to the realities of the ship and its methods can deliver a kind of freedom. When Odysseus is to be taken home to Ithaca, his departure from Scheria, the land of the Phaeacians, is a ritual of liberation. The king's herald 'shows him the way to the fast ship and the sand of the seashore.' The queen instructs her maids to provide him with a chest of clothes, a clean and washed mantle, bread and red wine. When they come to the ship, the men

> Spread a rug for Odysseus, and a linen sheet, out on deck,
> Laid at the stern of the ship, so that he might sleep there
> Undisturbed, and he went aboard and lay down in silence.

The crew gathers, sits on the benches, and with their oars start to take the ship out of harbour. As its hull begins to meet the swell of the sea,

> Sweet sleep fell upon Odysseus' eyes, the deepest
> And sweetest of sleeps, and like death in its quietness.

In the most perfect of ships, Odysseus finds himself liberated from the pains of life.

> As the stern lifted on the swell, the dark wave of her wake
> Foamed behind her, and she ran on safe and sure.
> Not even the circling hawk, the swiftest of winged birds,
> Could keep up with her, as she carried a man
> Equal to the gods in wisdom, one who in time past
> Had endured much and suffered many griefs at heart:
> The wars of men and the harrowing waters.
> Now on board, he slept in peace,
> Forgetful of all that he had suffered.

REVIEWS

Editors' Picks

Girlatee

By A M Juster, illustrated by Grant Silverstein
(Paul Dry Books, 55 pages)

Early in A M Juster's new children's picturebook, *Girlatee*, a female manatee named Grace is separated from her parents. Propelled from their favourite eelgrass haunt by a passing motorboat, she finds herself stranded on the beach. Rather than helping, nearby beachgoers spectate. Pulling out their phones, they jostle for pictures with the frightened creature.

In this, Juster smuggles a very timely message into this breezy, lavishly illustrated book. Are the devices on which we increasingly rely obstructing our empathy and intelligence? Are they making it more difficult to raise children with decency, care, imagination? If a children's book seems like the wrong place to be raising these questions, consider: fully a quarter of three- and four-year-olds in Britain own smartphones.

The illustrative etchings, by Grant Silverstein, underscore the point. A speedboat is depicted cruising past a sign that reads 'Slow: Manatees', thereby signalling to the reader that Grace's plight is not a random mishap: it is the result of people who should know better refusing their civic obligations for the sake of convenience and pleasure. On the beach, a child is shown posing for photos next to an older gentleman of strikingly similar appearance. Where do children learn bad behaviour? If they find scrolling more enjoyable than reading, have we given them reason to think otherwise?

Which is not to say that Juster's book is preachy or heavy-handed. He introduces his themes – the perils of tech, the seductive lure of voyeurism, our mandate to care for the natural world – with such rhyming grace that many readers may not notice. *Girlatee* succeeds in the primary task of a children's book, which is to transport its audience. The story follows a simplified hero's journey in which Grace is drawn from her home, an idyllic haven where she happily munches on 'fish, and octopi, and cranky crabs', into the human world with its innumerable dangers, and then back into the freedom of the water.

There is a passage in the Book of Job that can be puzzling on first reading. Throughout the book, Job has demanded an explanation from God for his sufferings. Finally, God manifests in a whirlwind and says, in effect, 'Have you seen the crocodile? Have you taken note of the ostrich?' The passage conveys something of God's inscrutability – the things that concern him are not the things that concern us – but also the extent of his love, the breadth of which surpasses human love. 'The compassion of man is toward his neighbour; but the compassion of the Lord is toward all flesh,' writes the author of the Wisdom of Sirach (18:13). To which the Wisdom of Solomon adds, 'For Thou lovest all things that are, and abhorrest nothing which Thou hast made' (11:24). When we care for other creatures, we extend compassion beyond its human limits and participate in divine love. By encouraging a love of creatures in children, Juster has done just that.

—*Boze Herrington*

Grant Silverstein, illustration from *Girlatee*.

Spring 2025

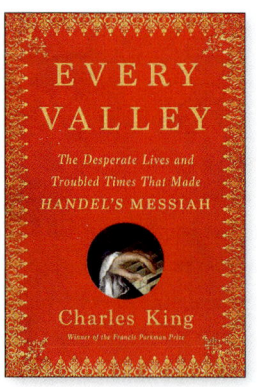

Every Valley
The Desperate Lives and Troubled Times That Made Handel's Messiah

By Charles King
(Doubleday, 352 pages)

On 13 April 1742, over 700 Dublin concertgoers squeezed into the Fishamble Street Music Hall, meant to only hold 600. They were about to hear a new work, an oratorio composed by Georg Frideric Handel. The oratorio put to music a collection of scripture passages that wove together the Christian story from the prophecies of the Hebrew Bible to the Gospels, all the way through to triumphal passages from the letters of Paul and the Book of Revelation. As its epigraph, Handel took a line from Virgil's 'Messianic Eclogue': *Majora canamus* – 'Let us sing of greater things.' As its name, Handel chose *Messiah*.

In *Every Valley*, Charles King, a professor at Georgetown University, describes this monumental performance in great detail. But his story begins many years earlier, charting Handel's rise to celebrity status in one of the most polarised ages of British history. Many, including Charles Jennens, the English landowner and patron of the arts who compiled the libretto for Handel's *Messiah*, quietly opposed the new Hanoverian regime granted the throne by the 1701 Act of Settlement. Handel, a German from Halle, however, had been Kapellmeister at the Hanoverian court before he (and the Hanoverians) permanently moved to London. Jennens's admiration of Handel's musical talent outweighed their political differences, and his determination to keep Handel writing despite setbacks in the composer's career made the eventual composition of *Messiah* possible.

King's book brilliantly weaves together the stories of several of Handel's and Jennens's contemporaries: Ayuba Diallo, an African Muslim man enslaved in the Americas who eventually makes his way to London, Thomas Coram, a philanthropic sea captain who works tirelessly into his old age to establish the first foundling hospital, and Jonathan Swift, the author of *Gulliver's Travels* and dean of Saint Patrick's Cathedral just down the road from where Handel's *Messiah* would first be performed. One of the characters most prominently featured in King's narrative is Susannah Cibber, a young alto soloist Handel hired last minute for *Messiah*'s debut. Four years before, her career had been shattered by a scandalous trial that had brought the sordid details of her personal life into public scrutiny. Nevertheless, as she sang one of the most famous arias of the oratorio, the audience sat gripped. 'He was despised and rejected of men, a man of sorrows, and acquainted with grief.' The words could have described her, the soloist, but instead they described Christ, the Messiah, who 'hath borne our griefs, and carried our sorrows.' When she finished her solo, Patrick Delany, chancellor of Christ Church Cathedral, declared from the audience, 'Woman, for this, be all thy sins forgiven.'

The stories that King recounts are all rooted in a particular time and place, but they consistently point to the reasons why Handel's *Messiah* still captures crowds today. Its biblical text remains as timely as ever: 'Why do the nations so furiously rage together?' Like the psalmist, Jennens's compilation does not attempt to provide a simple answer. Instead, it reminds us that 'the kingdom of this world is become the kingdom of our Lord and of his Christ; and he shall reign forever and ever.'

—*Alan Koppschall*

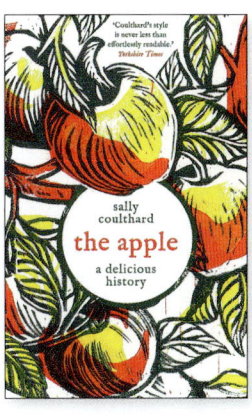

The Apple
A Delicious History

By Sally Coulthard
(Apollo, 368 pages)

I am privileged to live near an orchard. And not just any orchard but one that grows an assortment of apples bearing names that could have been plucked from a Dickens novel – Saint Edmund's Pippin, D'arcy Spice, Worcester Pearmain, and more. Though unusually diverse by modern standards, the 50 varieties grown by this orchard are a drop in the ocean compared to the 7,500 varieties worldwide, each expressing in their flavours and appearances the uniqueness of the place from which they originated.

Though the apple is world renowned, perhaps less well known is its rich and varied history. In her latest book, *The Apple: A Delicious History*, Sally Coulthard has trawled through the archives to uncover the intriguing, strange and sometimes absurd history of this most cherished and alluring fruit. With her witty and jovial prose, Coulthard puts the apple firmly on centre stage and showcases the surprising role this humble fruit has played in shaping the world today.

Coulthard takes us on a journey beginning where the apple originated, deep in the valleys of the Tien Shan mountains, across the Silk Road to Europe, where the apple captivated the ancient Greeks, and all the way to regal European courts where kings and queens from Charlemagne to Victoria fawned over the flavours of new varieties. We see how the fruit conquered the New World through the industrious exploits of the aptly named Johnny Appleseed, who may have planted a million trees and helped fuel westward expansion. And finally, we read how the apple became a truly global fruit as demand soared and new lands were sought where conditions were ripe for this fruit to flourish, Down Under and in the Far East.

Coulthard ends each chapter with a selection of apple-based recipes from ancient cookbooks, along with their often humorous backstories. We discover sweet appelbeignets, indulgent apple biffins, the contested history of apple crumble and the apparent use of apples to garnish a tortoise! One can't help but be tempted to try out some of these long-forgotten recipes for oneself.

But all this rich culinary and genetic diversity is under profound threat. Coulthard's final chapter

---

Traditional orchards, full of abundant wildlife and rare apples, are being condemned as uneconomical.

---

serves as a plea for help on behalf of the precious heritage varieties facing extinction, ironically because we are not eating enough of them. The supermarkets dominating our food system tend to stock only four or five varieties. Heritage apples rarely conform to the airbrushed aesthetic standards required by supermarkets, and are thus often neglected. Traditional orchards, full of abundant wildlife and rare apples, are being condemned as uneconomical. Our generation runs the risk that our part in this history will be losing, perhaps for good, the rich and wonderful diversity of the apple.

All is not hopeless. We can play a part in the apple's continual story – by purchasing local varieties from an orchard or perhaps even planting a heritage apple tree. We can perpetuate the remarkable variety of this wonderful fruit for future generations to enjoy. As Coulthard remarks, 'Only by celebrating the apple's incredible diversity and unique heritage will we ensure that its delicious history will continue.'

—*Hadden Turner*

Why I Love Metalworking

Teaching me his craft, my father showed me the value of manual work.

NORANN VOLL

I WAS IN THE FINAL YEAR of secondary school when I realised I was a peasant.

We were required to write a detailed family narrative for our Advanced Placement history class, and I was appalled: my grandfather, a Birmingham factory worker, had spoken in a lower-class accent and contemplated running away to Australia to make his life better because his grandfather was a highwayman who drank too much and fired his blunderbuss up the chimneys of respectable drawing rooms and laughed when the soot covered the clean houses.

And that was only one side of the family.

I'm not sure why this realisation bothered me so much, except that perhaps it collided with my growing teenage arrogance in my intellectual capabilities and general superiority to the rest of the world.

'We're just a bunch of proles,' I whined to my father. 'No class at all.'

'Blue-collar workers make the world go around, Nora,' he would remind me, knowing full well that my plumber brother and secretary and chef sisters were in earshot.

'And I shall not be one of them,' I would respond.

And so it went. I worked after school in an office, rode horses on the weekend, and studied in earnest to make straight As and so rewrite my family narrative of simplicity.

Norann's father welding a gate in Shropshire, England, in 1959 (left). Norann works with one of her sons in Danthonia Designs' metal shop (right).

My ordinarily patient father did not tolerate this for long. One evening, during our usual family session of answering his question, 'What did you do today to show kindness towards another person?' my father informed me that I was no longer going to work in the office after school but was to join him in the metal fabrication shop where he served as foreman.

I was not impressed.

Dad was steady and quiet. 'I sometimes feel like you despise me because I'm uneducated.'

That stung. My dad and I were close, and always had been. Our love and respect were mutual, but I couldn't deny that these had been fraying a little.

I knew Dad's background – he finished formal education at 14 and went away to an agricultural boarding school shortly afterwards. His next two years were filled with early rising, outdoor work on the school's farm, attending lectures and studying late into the night.

He learned metalworking alongside agriculture and took to it at once. Later, it became a livelihood when he worked for a business that manufactured farm gates. 'When you work with metal, you aren't at the mercy of the weather as you are with farming,' he said.

Dad taught welding to any of his children who wanted to learn. My brother was the first, and two of my sisters followed. 'Women make the best welders,' Dad said. 'Everything is neat and tidy the first time. No do-overs.'

I was not one of those women. I never had been. That sort of thing was quite beneath me.

Until now: on my first day in the fabrication shop, I was sheepish. I put my head down and buttoned up the protective jacket and put on the gloves and earplugs. Dad grinned and handed me a wire brush and showed me a cart of welded pieces. My job, he explained, was to prep these parts for painting, brushing the welds and inspecting them.

I scrubbed away at the welding spatter until it was smooth. Every weld had to be flawless, and the entire piece wiped clean with a cloth.

It wasn't difficult work, but it was monotonous and messy. The workshop was foreign: a cacophony of industrial noise, the unfamiliar smell of cutting fluid from the milling machines, and the burned metallic odours rising into the exhaust hoods above the welders. I was used to office banter, the clack of keyboards, the smell of coffee and toner, clean work surfaces, a light and airy mood, the feeling of getting important work done. Now I was in an earplugged cocoon, working with metal. My busy mind had to focus on new kinds of details: making rough places smooth. Over and over.

That first week turned into a month. A new set of the same metal parts greeted me every day, along with a cheeky grin from my dad. From the quality of the welds and amount of spatter, I soon learned who welded well and who was beginning. I began to befriend the other workers – Larry, a Vietnam veteran; Ruben, who had served time in prison; Chuck, the gentle giant whose daughter was about my age; and Shane, who had fallen on hard times and needed a steady job with an understanding boss.

By Christmas, I was enjoying the work. I used what I dubbed the 'noise of silence' to think. I had always loved hard work, but only on my terms. Working with metal put me in an environment of dust and grease and machines that millions of people enter each day in order to feed their families. Working with metal put me alongside people who didn't judge others by the kind of work they did but were thankful just to have work to do.

I worked in that fabrication shop until I had finished secondary school. And I returned as often as I could before I started college that autumn. It was addictive. Every time I walked in, there was

---

Norann Voll writes about discipleship, motherhood and feeding people. She lives with her husband, Chris, at Danthonia, a Bruderhof in rural Australia. They have three sons.

work to do. Every time I left, the pile of unfinished pieces was ready for the next part of their journey.

By rescuing me from my teenage smugness and conceit and placing me amidst metal and grime, my father was not romanticising manual labour

> 'God gave us brains and hands to work with. He does not place one above the other. But it's a gift when you can use both.'

nor suggesting I should bury my intellectual abilities. 'God gave us brains and hands to work with,' he told me. 'He does not place one above the other. But it's a gift when you can use both.'

THOSE DAYS ARE A MEMORY NOW. My dad died in 2007, just a few years after my husband and I moved with our two small sons to Australia, where the Danthonia Bruderhof community was just getting started. (Dad and Mum visited us for three precious months, in 2003, long enough for him to inspire the young men to help him make a steel-framed horse wagon, to fire up an old forge, and to fashion decorative hinges for a set of hardwood gates he built and installed at the site of the community's future cemetery. My very young sons 'helped' their grandfather.) But the years have not changed my love for working with metal, and I still do so every chance I get.

Danthonia Designs, the sign-making enterprise that provides our community's primary income here in Australia, involves a lot of metal fabrication. I may not know how to weld or operate a CNC router or press brake, but there are always plenty of welds to prep for painting – and no part moves up the supply chain until that's done. I've traded the inefficient wire brush of my youth for a pneumatic sander, with discs of varying grits to deliver the appropriate abrasion for the task. In the serenity of the noise of silence, I have time to be alone with my thoughts while I smooth out the world and fix the dents and straighten edges, readying an entire sign for its colour coat.

Some days I get to work alongside my sons when they're on break from university. They share my love of metal work – and have been blessed with learning opportunities to become skilled at it. One welds, another paints, but I always sand. It's the centre of the process, and the least glamorous.

My dad was a master craftsman not only of metal but also of the heart. He could hear the words that went unuttered, understand that imperfection is a given (starting with himself), smooth out a rough argument, visualise a finished product when everyone else saw scattered pieces, and nudge a wounded soul towards healing.

Naturally, I am still an unfinished piece, with plenty of rough corners and spattered welds still needing attention; we are each, after all, a work in progress. But I believe the gift my father gave me in that old workshop, now three decades ago, has done more to assist my 'finishing process' than anything else in my life.

In my childhood home, my siblings and I often heard our parents quote Rabindranath Tagore's famous lines: 'I slept and dreamt that life was joy. I awoke and saw that life was service. I acted and behold, service was joy.' That first evening walking home from the workshop with my dad, service-as-joy was the farthest thing from my mind.

'Nora,' he said gently, 'Often in life, we need to start over, from the bottom.' I looked up at him. 'You want to live a life of service, right?' I nodded. 'Well, service starts by doing the little things properly – sweeping the floor, taking out the trash, cleaning the toilet, or even brushing bits of metal. Until you can do those little things properly, you won't do anything larger well either.'

And that is why I love to work – with mind or metal. Or both.

Following the Clues

Detective stories help us discover meaning in life.

ALISTER McGRATH

How do we make sense of our universe? Of ourselves? Human beings seem inherently driven to seek meaning in life, sensing that something deeper lies beyond the horizons of our present experience that makes life worthwhile and fulfilling. The cultural anthropologist Clifford Geertz suggests that humanity 'cannot live in a world it is unable to understand.' We are 'symbolising, conceptualising, meaning-seeking animals,' who want to 'make sense out of experience, and give it some form and order.'

Sidney Paget, *'Holmes gave me a sketch of the events,'* illustration for *The Adventure of Silver Blaze*, 1892.

Human beings are always seeking meaning. Yet this 'meaning' proves elusive. It is not something that we observe; rather, it is something we have to uncover by *interpreting* what we observe. The universe stays silent about its own significance, compelling us, as its observers and interpreters, to discover 'some form and order.' P D James, who

> **The detective novel appeals to our underlying belief in the inherent rationality of the world around us on the one hand, and our capacity to uncover its underlying patterns on the other.**

created the investigator and poet Adam Dalgliesh of New Scotland Yard, famously remarked that 'what the detective story is about is not murder but the restoration of order.' Meaning is something that we uncover by following clues and discovering where they lead us.

Dorothy L Sayers, a prominent figure in the Golden Age of Detective Fiction, drew an explicit connection between fictional detectives, philosophy, and theology: like detectives, we are surrounded by a multitude of clues and must find the best framework to interpret them. The result is a new way of seeing things, enabling us to perceive the interconnectedness of these clues. The detective novel appeals to our underlying belief in the inherent rationality of the world around us on the one hand, and our capacity to uncover its underlying patterns on the other.

Sayers suggests that we experience a sense of accomplishment and satisfaction when we solve a mystery by uncovering the meaning of the clues. In a semi-autobiographical piece, she wrote about the 'satisfaction of plaiting and weaving together innumerable threads to make a pattern, a tapestry, a created beauty.' One of the best (and certainly one of the most enjoyable) examples of such a weaving together is the detective novel. We were not present to witness the mysterious death of Sir Charles Baskerville. Through careful analysis of the clues, however, Sherlock Holmes developed the most probable explanation of what truly occurred. We can look beyond the clues and discover the hidden thread that connects them.

One of the most familiar examples of this sense-making process is found in the natural sciences. Careful observation of our world leads to reflection on what theory – a term that denotes a way of 'seeing' or 'beholding' – can be found to connect and coordinate these clues. In the language of modern philosophy of science, theories are epistemic frameworks that we construct to make sense of phenomena. Isaac Newton's theory of gravitation was seen as a wonder of its age, demonstrating that the orbits of the planets around the sun and the falling of an apple to the ground were all interconnected. Yet, these are explanations of how our world *functions*, not interpretations of what it *means*.

Some argue that we should confine ourselves to scientific explanations of our world, yet this is both unnecessary and impoverishing. We need to use multiple intellectual toolkits to understand the world and our place within it. Science is one of them. But limiting ourselves to this single way of understanding our world impoverishes us. It restricts us to a partial vision of a rich and complex reality. It can't disclose or accommodate deep existential truths – such as purpose, meaning, or moral values. In fact, there are some who regard

---

Alister McGrath is a senior research fellow at the Faculty of Theology and Religion at Oxford University. He is best known for his textbook Christian Theology: An Introduction. *His latest book is* Why We Believe: Understanding Ourselves in a Complex World *(Simon & Schuster, 2025).*

Sidney Paget, *'He examined them minutely,'* illustration for *The Adventure of the Cardboard Box*, 1893.

any such quest for meaning as an outdated superstition, discredited by modern science.

In his book *The Atheist's Guide to Reality: Enjoying Life Without Illusions*, the atheist philosopher Alex Rosenberg asserts that science is 'our exclusive guide to reality', providing us with reliable certainties about our world and ourselves – such as his belief that there is 'no moral difference' between right and wrong. Given his rather dogmatic working assumptions, Rosenberg is entitled to draw this conclusion. If you rely solely on the natural sciences as your 'exclusive guide to reality', you will not be able to answer moral questions. Rosenberg is just being consistent here. But most of us feel deeply that moral questions are important!

Rosenberg provides his own somewhat unsatisfactory explanation for this human concern to do what is right. 'Why should I be moral? Because it makes you feel better than being immoral.' Happily, Rosenberg has a therapeutic solution for those who might be troubled by his radical exclusion of morality or meaning from their worlds. If this makes it impossible for you 'to get out of bed in the morning', then take some Prozac. (Other pharmacological solutions are, of course, available.)

This is where religious belief becomes relevant. It may seem strange to suggest that a fictional whodunit might help us make sense of life, but it really helps us appreciate the importance of following clues and seeing where they lead us. Like science, religious belief is about attempting to make sense of the clues we observe in our world and experience within us. For C S Lewis (an excellent representative of this approach), our sense of moral obligation and experiences of longing and desire are 'clues to the meaning of the universe.' Like their scientific counterparts, they open up new ways of thinking about ourselves and our world. Yet they operate at a different level. Lewis interprets human desire as a clue to our true nature and genuine needs. The realisation that nothing within the world ever seems able to satisfy our deepest longings is one clue among many others to the true meaning of the world.

Realising this is like a curtain being drawn aside for a moment, giving us a tantalising glimpse of a distant and beautiful landscape, leaving us with a painful longing to enter into it. We contemplate the splendour of the night sky, wondering whether the serene beauty of the stars could illuminate the mystery of human destiny. Is

> **Nature is studded with clues to our true meaning and destiny and fingerprinted with the presence of God.**

our true homeland out there, beyond this world? We appreciate the beauty of a glorious sunset while wondering whether the sense of beauty it evokes within us is a hint of another, more wonderful world that we have yet to discover.

For Lewis, the Christian faith has an explanatory capaciousness that makes sense of our observations and experiences, while also enabling us to develop moral values and an understanding of meaning that are grounded in this deeper vision of reality. Science helps us to understand how the world works, while religion helps us understand what it *means* and clarifies our place in the 'big picture' that it provides. It provides a lens through which we can perceive our world as it really is, offering a framework for interpreting its true meaning.

Not everything fits perfectly within this big picture. Like a landscape just before dawn, there are patches of mist and shadow that stubbornly linger, obscuring our vision. As Paul puts it, we presently 'see through a glass darkly' (1 Cor. 13:12), limited by human weakness and frailty. Yet we see enough to keep us going, reassuring us that there is indeed 'form and order' in life, even if we discern this only in part and imperfectly. Nature is studded with clues to our true destiny and fingerprinted with the presence of God.

In her remarkable book *Prisons We Choose to Live Inside*, Doris Lessing criticises what she calls the 'great over-simplifiers' who confine us in simplistic and shallow accounts of the world. These people simply ridicule anyone who suggests that things might be richer or more complicated than they are prepared to allow. They offer a superficial understanding of our world, a surface reading that overlooks its complexity and depth. Lessing argues that we needlessly walk into these prisons and close the door. But other, better ways of understanding our world are available; we can leave these imprisoning worldviews behind!

That's why we need to pay attention to the clues we find in the world around us and our inner experiences that challenge these reductive simplifications. They are what Peter L Berger terms 'signals of transcendence', indicating something deeper and richer that lies beyond our present vision. We need to break free from the constraints imposed by a diminished vision and limited understanding of human existence.

We must entertain the possibility that our sense of unfulfilled desire is not a mere illusion, the creation of a confused human mind. This sense of longing is one of many clues to our true identity and meaning, and a pointer to how we can achieve life in its fullness. Anselm of Canterbury (1033–1109), one of the greatest thinkers of the Middle Ages, points to how these clues can be resolved intellectually and fulfilled spiritually by realising that God is both the source and goal of this deep sense of yearning. As he writes in one of his prayers, 'Lord, give me what you have made me want; I praise and thank you for the desire that you have inspired; perfect what you have begun, and grant me what you have made me long for.'

TISH HARRISON WARREN

Stanley Hauerwas's Provocations

America's theologian isn't worried about the death of cultural Christianity.

This essay is the introduction to Jesus Changes Everything: A New World Made Possible *by Stanley Hauerwas (Plough, March 2025).*

STANLEY HAUERWAS feels larger than life. He's funny. He's insightful. He grew up a blue-collar kid in small-town Texas, which lends a grit and plainspokenness to his theological work that keeps us all on the hook. For him, theology is not an abstract game, a jostle amidst the experts with their jargon and fashionable truisms, a way to score points against others, or a way to bend the Christian story to fit our preferences. Instead, it is learning the story that teaches us to live.

Because of this, Hauerwas's work has had an unusually important, even intimate, impact on people's lives. I know more than one couple who decided to have children after reading Hauerwas

Henry Ossawa Tanner, *Miraculous Haul of Fishes*, oil on canvas, 1914.

Spring 2025   111

(and I wonder how many men and women Hauerwas will meet in the resurrection who will thank him for inspiring their parents). I – a descendant of dyed-in-the-wool Texans whose ancestral home had an heirloom war rifle hung over the mantel – became a pacifist because of Hauerwas. I have friends who went to seminary to study theology because of Hauerwas's work. His words change people.

Hauerwas is provocative, but not for provocation's sake. Instead, he calls us back to the disruptive words of Jesus, and to the church – to a community of ordinary people who are meant to learn to follow Jesus in the concreteness of our lives in a complex world. He is clear that following Jesus will always come at a cost and will disassemble most of our expectations about how our lives should turn out.

I FIRST CAME ACROSS Hauerwas's work sometime in the late 1990s, when I was in college. Reading him brought about something like a tectonic shift in my soul. His work changed the landscape. It changed how I saw the world.

I had grown up in a progressive city, Austin, Texas, in the nineties. I was also a Christian who knew about the so-called 'moral majority' committed to taking back 'family values.' In other words, I knew about the culture wars. And I was very cynical about all of it. I certainly never thought God was a Republican or a Democrat. But I didn't know where that left me, and I didn't know

---

Tish Harrison Warren is a priest in the Anglican Church in North America and the author of Liturgy of the Ordinary *and* Prayer in the Night, *among other books. She was formerly a weekly newsletter writer for the* New York Times. *She lives with her husband and three children in Austin, Texas, USA.*

Henry Ossawa Tanner, *Christ and his Disciples on the Road to Bethany,* oil on canvas, ca. 1902.

how to faithfully navigate American society as a Christian. I had little interest in devoting myself to the political left or right, but I was also uninspired by the idea of being a stubborn moderate trying to walk a centrist tightrope, which seemed antithetical to how Jesus lived his life. (Very few moderates are tortured and executed by empires.) In short, I lacked a Christian political theology and was sceptical of the options the culture (including church culture) seemed to offer.

Hauerwas's insistence that the first social task of the church is to *be* the church oriented me like a lost hiker who discovers a trusty compass. The notion that the church is an alternative community that embodies a different sort of kingdom, and that an allegiance to that kingdom is our truest political and social responsibility, came as a breath of fresh air.

Over the 20 years since, as I've grown older, been ordained, and continued to seek to follow Jesus, I've come to see that what it means for the church to be the church is a pretty complicated question. This is why Hauerwas's voice is needed now more than ever – to help the church recall who she is and learn how to be the church.

The misguided days of decades past with 'moral majority' Christians seem almost quaint now, given the way American politics have metastasised into a vitriolic, quasi-religious conflict. Many Christians see those on the other side of the aisle as their mortal enemies. Yet both the right and the left seem to tacitly agree that the radical calls in the Sermon on the Mount to meekness, mourning, turning the other cheek and loving enemies are outdated. Some Christians explicitly say that turning the other cheek doesn't work anymore, that we have to fight back now.

But Hauerwas makes clear that turning the other cheek has never 'worked', if by 'working' we mean creating a nice life for ourselves or for our children that is free of suffering and sacrifice, a life that fits neatly into the cultural expectations and political categories of our moment.

The call of Jesus to, for instance, turn the other cheek and love our enemies only makes sense if it is embodied by a community dedicated to being an embassy of the kingdom of God in wider society. And this will mean that we are, as Paul says, 'aliens and strangers.' And, whatever else that means, it implies we will never feel quite at home.

For me, Hauerwas is at his most bracing when he says that to deprive Christians of suffering is to tell them that they cannot follow Jesus to the cross. The church today is weak, he says, because of 'sentimentality', our unwillingness to allow ourselves or our children to suffer because of our convictions. We use whatever means necessary to avoid the cross.

Hauerwas also reminds us that, regardless of political party, any attempt by Christians to grasp control will inevitably give way to a worldliness that devolves into pride and violence. The sacrifices required by both war and violence are 'counter-liturgies' to the sacrifice of the altar, he says. Jesus' sacrifice on the cross and our participation in that once-for-all sacrifice every time we receive the Eucharist render the human sacrifice of violence false and idolatrous.

We can be 'disciples' of Jesus – rather than mere 'admirers' of him – only insofar as we recognise that the story that forms us insists that Jesus is already in control. We don't have to prove this in a show of power or through political means.

Instead, we as a church are to live into the story of what he's already accomplished on the cross. Jesus – not us or America or the West or democratic politics – has brought the kingdom. Indeed, he *is* the kingdom enfleshed, and he demonstrates this, surprisingly, through his utter vulnerability.

All of this is profoundly counter-cultural. It's even transgressive. And Hauerwas is, in the best sense, transgressive, not because he's saying something novel but simply because he dares (and dares us) to take the scriptures seriously enough to be disturbed by them. Most of us Christians, particularly in the West, often contort the teachings of Jesus to fit into our own quest for the 'good life.' We make God our ally in self-actualisation and realising the American dream, and buffer ourselves against the stark consequences of his teachings.

> 'Jesus does not want Christians. At least not in the sense of people who simply profess certain beliefs about him. As followers of Jesus, our beliefs cannot be separated from how we live. The temptation to separate Christian "truths" from the lives we live is due to fear of being held accountable and leads to a duplicity that gnaws at our faith. Jesus teaches that it is by our fruits that we, and he, will be known. The truth of the story we find in the Gospels is known only through the kind of lives it produces.' —Stanley Hauerwas

But if transgression in our culture is seen mostly in terms of individuals being 'true to themselves', Hauerwas clearly calls people away from individualism and to a specific community. Nothing else Hauerwas says will make sense unless we believe that the church really matters. How we view the church matters. 'The church does not have a social ethic,' Hauerwas argues; 'the church *is* a social ethic.' Our ability to welcome the vulnerable, the disabled, and children; to speak truth; to practise generosity; to honour the limits and holiness of human bodies; to live 'out of step' with the world; and to love our enemies is the embodiment of an ethic birthed out of the resurrection. This kind of discipleship isn't a strategy for winning an election, having a picture-perfect family, or getting a raise. It is, however, as Hauerwas says, living 'with the grain of the universe', and is therefore the strange way of abundant life.

The way the church embodies this ethic is contextual and improvisational. While in some ways 'being the church' is a universal and perennial call to all generations, the details and practices of this call will change according to the needs of our neighbours and the failures or strengths of a particular church at a given time. Of course, all of this must be discerned through the power of the Holy Spirit.

What it means for the church to be the church, however, is not to pick a side in the culture wars; nor is it to suss out some moderate position; nor is it to be apolitical or quietist. Instead, we learn together, in conversation with the church throughout time, to embody an alternative community that can approach all of life in a different way, a way shaped by the story and practices of creation, fall, redemption, and consummation.

When Christ came into the world as the king of a kingdom that is not of this world – a kingdom based in truth and not in power – neither Rome nor the Hellenistic civilisations around the church had any categories with which to understand this. Early Christians had no interest in directly supporting or upholding the empire, and they did not participate in the pagan temple sacrifices. In some ways, then, they may seem to have been apolitical.

But, as Hauerwas writes, the refusal of Christians to kill is what required the church to be political. The early church was interested in a radically different sort of peace than that offered by allegiance to any earthly cause. And this strange political community ended up seeding the world with the gospel.

We, like the earliest Christians, are still called to resist the political categories, assumptions, and demands of our day. What the church does jointly when it gathers for worship is its foremost political action. Proclaiming 'Jesus is Lord' has profound (though non-partisan) political ramifications. We are citizens of another kingdom, called to demonstrate the ethics of that kingdom.

H AUERWAS BOLDLY CALLS US to this vision and charts a path of what it may look like in our own moment and culture. He dismantles Christian nationalism, which seems to be as rampant as ever, yet he also rebukes Christian progressivism and the ways it seeks to make the gospel more palatable to our culture. He calls all of us into something completely different: a community shaped by the cross of Christ, a community that welcomes others without losing itself, a community that makes no sense to this world because it is formed by the Spirit of God.

Hauerwas also reminds us that as a church we must be formed by a story. In other words, he reminds us that theology matters – that, as he points out, poorly trained Christian pastors and leaders can do as much harm as poorly trained surgeons. In one talk he gave recently, I heard him skewer the oft-repeated truism that 'people don't care how much you know till they know how much you care.' The church and the pastoral

> 'The most interesting, creative political solutions we Christians have to offer our troubled society are not new laws, advice to policymakers, or increased funding for social programmes – although we may support such efforts from time to time. The most creative social strategy we have to offer is to be the church. Here we show the world a manner of life that it can never achieve through social coercion or governmental action. We serve the world by showing it something that it is not, namely, a place where God is forming a family out of strangers.' —Stanley Hauerwas

office are being dumbed down so that the pastor is simply a nice counsellor or therapist, and the church's job is mostly to make everyone feel happy and uplifted.

Hauerwas has no time for this kind of benign faith. (If one is primarily after agreeable spiritual uplift, I'd recommend avoiding Hauerwas.) He insists that we think theologically: that our minds and our whole lives – and our approach to every part of life – be deeply and meaningfully shaped by the story of Jesus. Sit with his words long enough and they become something like a solvent for clichés and platitudes. And this is needed now more than ever. People today often want to reduce the Christian faith to a debate that can fit into a hashtag. But true theology, as Hauerwas brilliantly says, makes believing in Jesus 'more difficult.' He understands that we have to struggle to be shaped by the story of Jesus, and that if we do not, we will inevitably be shaped by other, lesser stories. Poor theology, then, isn't just some kind of spiritual faux pas. It deforms the church as a community. It produces cruelty and makes the development of Christian virtue impossible. Bad theology makes us into admirers of Jesus, not disciples.

What Hauerwas does well is bring to light the deep logic that is often shared between those who seemingly hold divergent, partisan views. He challenges things we usually take for granted, things like individual autonomy and rights, the idolatry of the nuclear family, the importance of personal identity, and the sentimentality of romance. And, for that matter, the sentimentality of 'faith' as well. In challenging the deep logic held by all 'sides' in our culture, Hauerwas defies easy thinking and explodes easy answers. He instead insists that Christianity demands a rigour in thought and speech that makes truth-telling possible. Whatever else the words of Hauerwas do, they always make me think – and they teach me to think differently.

Hauerwas is impossible to categorise theologically. He is a Catholic-Anabaptist-Anglican. Sort of. But this is not because he is noncommittal or haphazard about the need for a local church. It's because what Hauerwas offers is the kind of catholic faith that is shaped by a broad tradition of Christian thinking. His vision for the church, then, will challenge everyone.

Hauerwas reminds me that Jesus came to create a people, a polity, on earth. This is part of the gospel. The church is part of Christ's continuing story in the world. And Hauerwas also reminds us that it is always possible – even now – for the church to repent and be reborn. In fact, he says this post-Christendom age, when the church is quickly losing status and favour in the West, may be the best time to rediscover what it means to be Christians.

My husband and I often describe our society now as 'post-Christendom *and* pre-Christian.' This suggests, with hope, that people may be able to hear the gospel anew. It means that God is still after our hearts and the hearts of our neighbours, friends and fellow church members. As the delusion of an erstwhile 'Christian West' fades, and as the number of those reporting no religious affiliation rises, disciples of Jesus may seek to proclaim and practise the gospel without the trappings of respectability, power, political captivity and nationalism that have so long defined and malformed it. This is a big project, one big enough that it is worth giving our lives to. And in this project Stanley Hauerwas continues to be a key voice helping us chart the way of Jesus – to be the church Jesus created and loves.

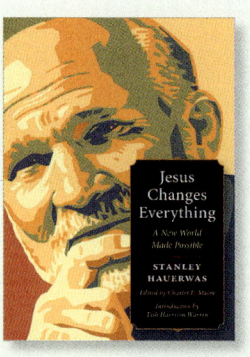

Jesus Changes Everything
A New World Made Possible

Stanley Hauerwas
Edited by Charles E. Moore
Introduction by Tish Harrison Warren

These accessible readings selected from Hauerwas's seminal books will introduce a timely, prophetic voice to another generation of followers of Jesus tired of religion as usual.

Softcover, 168 pages

~~£9.99~~ **£6.99 (with subscriber discount)**

To order, simply scan the QR code and enter PQ30 at checkout.

Ora et Labora

Benedict of Nursia teaches us to fuse prayer and work.

WILLIAM P HYLAND

Italy in the late fifth century was in many ways a difficult place. The Roman imperial government had collapsed recently and had been replaced by a Gothic kingdom. The new rulers were Arian Christians, who denied the full divinity of Christ and were deeply distrusted by the Catholic population. Whatever stability existed was often disrupted by Byzantine armies trying to reconquer the peninsula for a Roman empire now ruled from distant Constantinople. Into this world of violence and disorder, a young aristocrat who would become known to history as Saint Benedict of Nursia was born (ca. 480). We are told that after a brief sojourn in Rome to pursue higher studies as a young man, he was disgusted by the way of life there and left to live with a hermit in the countryside for a time. Eventually he pursued a life of prayer and solitude in a cave in Subiaco, and then moved on to found many different monasteries, most famously Monte Cassino. Pope Gregory the Great wrote his life, where he discusses many miracles associated with Benedict. He died in 547.

Sometime in the later years of his life, Benedict produced his Rule for monks. Monasticism had been flourishing since the later third century, and Benedict was in many ways the heir to this tradition. He was influenced by the Desert Fathers of Egypt, the Greek Basil the Great and the Latin John Cassian, among others, and he also drew from a long text called the *Rule of the Master*. But Benedict's Rule is very much his

---

William P Hyland teaches church history in the School of Divinity at the University of St Andrews, Scotland.

A medal of Saint Benedict.

own work of genius, distilling and combining Eastern Christian wisdom and a Roman talent for structure and organisation. Compared to earlier monastic writings, it stresses balance and moderation in matters of asceticism. And while he acknowledges that one could eventually become a hermit, this is only the case if one proves himself for many years living communally under the authority of a spiritual father known as an abbot. During the 1,500 years of its existence, his Rule has become the leading guide in Western Christianity for men and women living in Benedictine communities, including many offshoots, such as the Cistercians and Trappists. Why has it proven to be so successful and influential? Compared to previous monastic legislation, the Rule provides a moderate path focusing on the spiritual development of monks in a community environment. All property is shared, and all are taken care of based upon their needs. It provides a framework to establish order and guidance under a spiritual father to support and strengthen the individual's development in Christian holiness on the path to eternal life. The Rule opens with a hortatory prologue, in which Benedict sets forth the main principles of the religious life. Drawing on military metaphors familiar to his Roman audience, he stresses the renunciation of one's own will, and arming oneself 'with the strong and noble weapons of obedience under the banner of the true king Christ the Lord.' Benedict famously sets out to establish a 'school for the Lord's service' in which 'the way to salvation' shall be taught, so that by persevering in the monastery till death his disciples may 'through patience share in the passion of Christ that [they] may deserve also to share in his kingdom.' He then sets out moral and other teachings over 73 chapters, such as the famous 12 steps of humility; how the liturgy should be organised; the central importance of hospitality; and the administrative structure of the abbey, including the election of the abbot and the consultative nature of the abbot's leadership.

The Rule organises the day into regular periods of communal and private prayer, spiritual reading, and manual labour. The heart of the day is the cycle of liturgical prayer, which mainly consists of recitation of the Psalms and other scriptural readings, and is organised around various hours, going from the predawn prayers until compline, the last liturgy before retiring for sleep. These liturgical hours frame other times that are set aside for various types of manual labour and spiritual reading (*lectio divina*), the slow, prayerful reflection on scripture followed by contemplation.

The structure of the monastic day represents a profound attitude towards all human activity. Every action was intended to be approached in a manner that quite simply glorified God. The three vows required of a monk, namely ongoing conversion of life, obedience to the Rule and abbot and finally stability – that is, a commitment to persevere in the community until death – were the means to achieve this posture of receptivity to God's grace at every moment in the lifelong journey of holiness. All of life was meant to be an offering, so that 'God might be glorified in all things.' The activities that made up the day were meant to mutually nourish each other, and ultimately they were not separate silos. For example, the Divine Office, the formal time of

Saint Benedict resuscitating a boy, in a detail from a 15th-century illuminated antiphonary.

but should do everything with moderation and according to the abbot's orders. Above all, let him be humble. If goods are not available to meet a request, he will offer a kind word in reply, for it is written: 'A kind word is better than the best gift.'[2]

This is a profound expression of the Benedictine spirit! Essentially all things belonging to the monastery are sacred vessels, with the tools of the fields and kitchen to be no less cherished and cared for than the vessels used for the Eucharist. All work is sacred. And there is nothing wasteful or extravagant. The cellarer must be moderate, attentive and obedient to the bigger picture; humble, but most

> **All things belonging to the monastery are sacred vessels, with the tools of the fields and kitchen to be no less cherished and cared for than the vessels used for the Eucharist.**

of all kind. In later centuries, intellectual work and teaching, copying manuscripts, musical composition, art and architecture took their place alongside farming, crafts and other forms of manual labour for many – if not most – Benedictines. It is incredible how, in their own quiet and unexpected way, these 'byproducts' of Benedict's vision of *ora et labora* helped create a new medieval Christian civilisation, as John Henry Newman eloquently observed:

> Saint Benedict found the world, physical and social, in ruins, and his mission was to restore it in the way not of science, but of nature, not as if setting about to do it, not professing to do it by any set time, or by any rare specific, or by any series of strokes, but so quietly, patiently, gradually, that often till the work was done, it was not known to be doing. It was a restoration rather than a visitation, correction or conversion. The new work which he helped to create was a growth rather than a structure. Silent men were observed about the country, or discovered in the forest, digging, clearing and building; and other silent men, not seen, were sitting in the cold cloister, tiring their eyes and keeping their attention on the stretch, while they painfully copied and recopied the manuscripts which they had saved. There was no one who contended or cried out, or drew attention to what was going on, but by degrees the woody swamp became a hermitage, a religious house, a farm, an abbey, a village, a seminary, a school of learning and a city.[3]

These developments grew organically out of life in the monastery, which focused upon the daily round of liturgy and spiritual reading, and Benedict in his genius saw this as the source and nourishment of all genuine Christian activity. But this also had to manifest itself constantly in good actions, some of them large and dramatic, but most seemingly mundane and ordinary. One fruit of this was an intense feeling and obligation of hospitality towards travellers and refugees of all sorts. Italy in the sixth century witnessed a depressing and relentless stream of war, famine and desolation. In such a context, Benedict continued to insist, each visitor should be treated as if he or she were Christ, upon the necessity of unconditional love of neighbour, respect for the most minute aspects of human dignity, and a love and veneration for all of creation. This aspect of self-offering, or oblation, is needed now more than ever before, in addition to the perpetual calling of all the saints, both known and unknown, whether in monasteries or not.

---

2. *RB 1980: The Rule of St. Benedict in Latin and English*, trans. by Timothy Fry OSB (Liturgical Press, 1981), 229.

3. John Henry Newman, 'The Mission of St Benedict' (1858).

Artwork by Blair Barlow. Used by permission.

liturgical prayer, was referred to as 'the work of God.' Spiritual reading was referred to as 'divine reading.' And manual labour, always preceded by a quiet prayer, was to be offered up to God. Considered in this way, we see that Benedict intended for *all of life to be a prayer*. Equally, the Benedictine motto *ora et labora*, 'pray and work', is not ultimately referring to separate activities, but rather the integration of the two in all activities.

THE MEDIEVAL HAGIOGRAPHICAL tradition throughout the centuries, though also emphasising dramatic ascetic feats and martyrdom, has given a central place to the importance of the humblest actions in our spiritual lives. This was also the case in Pope Gregory the Great's sixth-century narrative of the life of Benedict. As in all medieval hagiographical literature, miracles performed by God through the intercession of the saint form an important part of the story. According to Gregory, the very first miracle Benedict performed was to repair a tray that his nurse accidentally broke. He writes:

> The poor woman burst into tears; she had just borrowed this tray and now it was ruined. Benedict, who had always been a devout and thoughtful boy, felt sorry for his nurse when he saw her weeping. Quietly picking up both the pieces, he knelt down by himself and prayed earnestly to God, even to the point of tears. No sooner had he finished his prayer than he noticed that the two pieces were joined together again, without even a mark to show where the tray had been broken. Hurrying back at once, he cheerfully reassured his nurse and handed her the tray in perfect condition.[1]

According to Gregory, Benedict would go on to prophesy before kings, heal the sick and even raise the dead, but I am not sure if those great works of the Spirit are any more beautiful than this prayerful and heartfelt desire to reach out and help a fellow human being in emotional distress. His life and his Rule are full of concern for the little things, such as caring for the sick and extending hospitality to all. Many examples could be given, but Benedict's description of the duties of the cellarer, the official in charge of the goods of the monastery, is typical:

> He must show every care and concern for the sick, children, guests and the poor, knowing for certain that he will be held accountable for all of them on the day of judgement. He will regard all utensils and goods of the monastery as sacred vessels of the altar, aware that nothing is to be neglected. He should not be prone to greed, nor be wasteful and extravagant with the goods of the monastery,

---

1. *Life and Miracles of St. Benedict: Book Two of the Dialogues*, trans. by Odo Zimmermann OSB and Benedict Avery OSB (Liturgical Press, 1949), 3.

An eighth-century manuscript of Saint Benedict's Rule.